Praise for Lessons to Grow a Billion-Dollar Company

"Samih Darwazah generously shares his experience and insights into the business challenges and opportunities in Jordan and the Middle East. The valuable story of one of our region's most successful executives, whose life, work, success, and philanthropy are a source of great pride."

**—Her Majesty Queen Noor Al Hussein,
The Hashemite Kingdom of Jordan**

"A potent blend of conventional, down-to-earth, old-fashioned wisdom and deep, incisive insights into the workings of modern business and economy, coupled with a determinedly modernist outlook, make this advice to young people invaluable. And as a rags-to-riches story, it is narrated with humility and wit, with integrity, generosity of spirit, and compassion shining through, so as to make the account a veritable inspiration."

—Khalil Hindi, president, Birzeit University

"Samih Darwazah is a world-class entrepreneur. In this volume he demonstrates that he is also a consummate teacher. In twenty-three lessons, he teaches the attributes and values upon which he has built his company and conducted his life. His journey has been one of risk-taking, perseverance, high personal standards, strong business ethics, respect of others, and love of family. He teaches us a true prescription for success. Great read. Great man."

**—Thomas F. Patton, PhD, president emeritus,
St. Louis College of Pharmacy**

"Samih Darwazah's compelling story of a childhood interrupted by sectarian conflict is all too common in the Middle East. But how he transformed those challenges into opportunities and worked his way to the heights of entrepreneurial success is far from common: it is extraordinary.

"*Lessons to Grow a Billion-Dollar Company* shows how Darwazah channeled the courage and determination he learned from his youthful ordeals into founding a company and leading it to success in the global pharma arena. He has learned many lessons along the way, and now he is sharing them with the world.

"Darwazah takes the best of Western business practices—transparency, environmental awareness, worker safety, concern for public health—and integrates these with the best of Arab customs and business etiquette, emphasizing trust, honor, conviviality, generosity, and strong family ties.

"Captivating the reader with personal anecdotes that are illustrative of the twenty-three lessons in the book, Darwazah's engaging style makes for delightful reading. Indeed, many of the lessons are informative for an audience much wider than the world of business. These are words of wisdom from which many can profit.

"A distinguished graduate of the American University of Beirut, another amalgamation of East meets West, Darwazah epitomizes the school motto: "that they may have life, and have it more abundantly." Having lived his life abundantly, Darwazah imparts the lessons he has learned to future generations, so they may do the same."

—Peter Dorman, president, American University of Beirut

Lessons to Grow a Billion-Dollar Company

Mixing Family & Business

Samih T. Darwazah

West-Ward Pharmaceuticals
A Hikma Company

Book design by:
Arbor Books, Inc.
www.arborbooks.com

Printed in the United States of America

Lessons to Grow a Billion-Dollar Company:
Mixing Family & Business
Samih T. Darwazah

1. Title   2. Author   3. Business/Memoir

Library of Congress Control Number: 2014950365

ISBN 13: 978-0-9907855-0-7

For my big family of employees who helped me build Hikma.

TABLE OF CONTENTS

ACKNOWLEDGMENTS

I would like to thank my lovely wife, Samira, for standing by me and supporting me with a smile for all these years. Samira, you are my rock, my better half, and the most perfect partner anyone could want.

Special thanks to my daughter, Hana, and granddaughter, Tamara, who spent many hours patiently editing this book. Without their input, it would not have been possible.

Samih Darwazah
November 4, 2013

LESSON ONE

Be Courageous and Strong

I watched with growing concern the images flashing across my television screen. Our crisis management team was already on standby, closely monitoring the situation.

Days earlier, on Tuesday, January 25, 2011, a small number of demonstrators had begun antigovernment protests in Cairo, Egypt. Within hours many took to the Internet and social media, and their words inspired the crowds to swell to tens of thousands in cities across the nation. Violent clashes with the police and military soon followed.

By Wednesday morning Egypt's president, Hosni Mubarak, had ordered police to fire concussion grenades, tear gas, and rubber bullets into the crowds to make them disperse. That served only to fuel the protesters' anger.

Weeks earlier the same type of massive street demonstrations had occurred in Tunisia. The riots had grown in size and violence, culminating just days ago in the ouster of the country's president, Zine El Abidine Ben Ali.

What we didn't realize at the time was the events in Tunisia and Egypt were the start of the Arab Spring, a series of violent protests throughout the Middle East and North Africa (MENA) region calling for massive government changes.

Most people in the Middle East, where I'm from, have had to deal with wars and civil unrest. For the most part, we take these things in stride, watching events on TV with interest but in a detached, "yes, that again" sort of way.

Then there are the wars that affect you personally because you and those you love are in the middle of fighting. When uprisings strike too closely and you've been through a similar event, you can experience a bit of post-traumatic stress as memories long buried rise to haunt you once again.

That was the case in 1975, when the company I was working for reassigned me to Beirut—a vibrant, wealthy, culturally rich city often described as the Paris of the Middle East due to its strong French influence. When civil war between Muslims and Christians broke out in Lebanon on April 13 of that year, shortly after my family and I had moved there, the conflict quickly escalated, forcing us to pack up and flee the country. I have to admit the fighting unnerved me not only because it was physically close to us but because it brought back uncomfortable memories of the wars in the Middle East I'd experienced as a child and teenager.

The war in Lebanon turned out to be very bloody. By the time it ended fifteen years later, 120,000 people had been killed in the fighting.

The riots in Egypt in 2011 were just as personal for me. I had eight hundred employees there, and I had to find out if they were safe.

Hikma Pharmaceuticals, the company I'd founded more than thirty years earlier, has production facilities in the United States, Europe, and countries in the MENA region. We'd tried for years to get a foothold in Egypt, but government regulations made it difficult for foreign firms to do business there. Finally, in 2007, we'd purchased a majority share of Egypt's Alkan Pharma, and that allowed us to start expanding.

For us medical needs supersede a country's political interests. We supply pharmaceuticals to the medical community: hospitals, clinics, doctors, and nurses. People need our products to feel better, to heal, to survive—and that's more important than whoever is the latest ruler or what ideology he or she holds. When uprisings begin I, along with my employees, try not to get involved in that aspect.

Almost 60 percent of Hikma's revenue comes from the MENA region. Dealing with disturbances is the reality of living and doing business in that part of the world. But money isn't our most important concern. It's the safety of Hikma's employees. We don't intentionally send our people into war zones, but occasionally they find themselves in the middle of sudden chaos. It goes without saying our employees need a healthy dose of courage to stay strong through situations like that.

Early on the morning of Friday, January 28, Egyptian government officials cut the nation's Internet access along with text and mobile-phone services, hoping if people didn't have access to social media sites and couldn't communicate with each other instantaneously, they wouldn't be able to organize large-scale protests. It didn't work. Hundreds of thousands of people took to the streets, and now they were even more furious.

On Sunday, after five days of violence, Egyptian bank officials told managers not to open because they were concerned the continued runs on their branches would deplete them of all available cash. Banks typically keep only 3 to 10 percent of their total deposits in cash reserves in their vaults. Some of Egypt's eighty-four million people had already begun clearing out their accounts, and officials knew if the banks didn't close their doors they'd soon be out of cash.

The nation's currency, the Egyptian pound, plunged in value, as did the stock market.

I told my assistant to make plans for me to go to Egypt. Some of my family and corporate managers objected since only three months earlier I'd celebrated my eightieth birthday, and they felt the trip might be too grueling for me. But as far as I was concerned, not going wasn't even an option. I was determined to get to my employees.

The problem was flights into and out of the country weren't reliable. On Monday, Egypt Air cancelled their flights.

Industries started shutting down as workers called for massive strikes. The uprisings forced us to stop production for a week, and that cost us about three months' worth of sales in Egypt, but we plan for things like this. We made up the losses quickly because of the way our company is structured, with facilities and clients spread throughout the world.

The price of food skyrocketed in Egypt at the few stores that dared to stay open, but since the banks weren't open many people didn't have the cash to pay for the goods. A week after the banks had closed, they briefly reopened for half a day, but the lines to get in stretched for blocks, with hours of waiting time. The banks converted Egyptian pounds into US dollars for as many people as they could.

We knew we had to get cash to our employees. The ATMs were depleted, and the banks were still closed, as were most stores and restaurants. Unless employees had credit cards and could find places to accept them, they wouldn't be able to buy food.

The bank we used for our employees' payroll was right next door to our facility. Our Egyptian general manager, Dr. Hassan Shafick, convinced the bank manager, whom he knew personally, to give us the cash we needed to cover our payroll. Our employees are so invested in the local communities and have personal friendships with so many well-connected people, they're able to pick up the phone and quickly arrange things such as that.

Those local ties also helped us get paid. Despite the chaos the country was experiencing, our clients in the government sector didn't delay or stop payments for the medications we were providing.

We treat each of our pharmaceutical manufacturing plants as a local company and hire as many people from that area as possible, including for management positions. Locals know their country and its needs better than anyone brought in from a foreign country. They're also better equipped to help those who become ill or wounded during national emergencies or civil unrest.

Over the next three weeks, Egypt's bloody riots, arson, and looting would leave almost nine hundred dead and more than three thousand injured.

On the morning of Friday, February 11, as protesters marched on the presidential palace, President Hosni Mubarak and his family escaped by helicopter to the Almaza Airbase. Then, after transferring to the presidential jet, they fled to Sharm el-Sheikh, a city on the southern tip of the Sinai Peninsula. At 6:00 p.m. the vice president announced Mubarak had resigned. After ruling

Egypt for thirty years, he'd been forced from office the same way Tunisia's president had.

I flew into Egypt four days later and, after checking in at the Four Seasons Hotel in Cairo, had my driver take me to our plant, located about twenty miles away in 6th of October City. The area was named after the 1973 date when Egypt, along with other Arab states, made a surprise attack on Israel. (Arabs refer to the war as the October War while Jews refer to it as the Yom Kippur War because October 6 that year was Yom Kippur, their high holy day that requires fasting for twenty-four hours.)

6th of October City is home to one of the largest industrial zones in Egypt. Our Hikma plant is located in the area known as the Second Industrial Zone.

After touring our facilities, I joined my employees in the cafeteria for a lunch of *kushari*, a popular dish made of pasta, lentils, and tomatoes. I wanted to hear their perspectives on the political situation, and they told me they were pleased with the outcome of events and equally as happy to be back at work. They were picking up the pieces of their lives and moving ahead. I told them we were planning to build a new pharmaceutical plant in order to expand Hikma Egypt. I also added they were all going to get raises.

On February 15, the same day I arrived in Egypt, antigovernment protests began in Libya and quickly escalated, eventually leading to the overthrow and death of that country's dictator, Colonel Muammar Gaddafi.

Again we were concerned for our Hikma personnel. Some of our Jordanian employees working in Libya felt the situation was becoming too dangerous for them to stay, so we coordinated with the Jordanian embassy in Tripoli and the Jordanian foreign ministry to evacuate them rapidly.

Hikma has a crisis-management team that keeps an eye on volatile situations around the world. Not only does the team make sure our local employees are safe when a situation gets too dangerous, but they're also equipped to evacuate foreign employees swiftly to their home countries.

The Arab Spring wasn't the first time our employees in the

MENA region had to deal with political unrest and war. During the Israel-Hezbollah War in Lebanon in July 2006, fighting forced the Beirut-Rafic Hariri International Airport to shut down for a few days, meaning medical supplies couldn't get into the country. Our Hikma team members who lived in Lebanon were able to provide much-needed drugs to hospitals and clinics from the supplies we had in our warehouses. We were glad to help those who needed us in a time of crisis even though we weren't paid for those medications until the situation stabilized more than a month later.

During the first Gulf War in 1990, we learned the medical community in Iraq was in dire need of medications and doctors to help sick and wounded civilians. At the same time, we discovered a delegation of Algerian doctors wanted to offer their assistance, but Saddam Hussein's government was refusing to allow any foreigners into the country.

My son, Mazen, contacted Saddam's Ministry of Health and arranged for Hikma to deliver three truckloads of antibiotics and anesthesia along with a convoy of Algerian doctors. They were the only ones Saddam allowed into the country.

Courage under fire can strengthen you and lead you to accomplish great things. Eighteen years later, in November 2008, when Mazen was accompanying Jordan's King Abdullah II on his first official visit to Algeria as a reigning monarch, he happened to run into one of the brave doctors who'd been part of that mission of mercy to help wounded Iraqi civilians. The doctor had become Algeria's minister of health.

Courage and Strength

If there's one thing I've learned, it's how to survive when my entire world is literally crashing and burning around me.

Wars can really interrupt a life. More than once political upheavals have left me a refugee, and security isn't guaranteed anywhere in the world. Life has shown me countries will fall and institutions will fail. It's not a matter of if but when. Some will last longer than others, but no matter how solid they appear, they're on borrowed time. Whether you consider the great conquering and nation-ruling powers of the Babylonians or even the Persian, Roman, Parthian, or Ottoman Empires, they all ended. Financially and politically the world's a shaky place these days. That's why you need to be courageous and strong—not only to survive life but also to be successful in your career, whether it's moving up through the ranks of a large corporation, opening your own business, or even growing your company into an international corporation—all three of which I've done.

For some having courage and strength may come naturally, possibly as a result of the preparation for life they went through as children and teenagers. For others those character traits may seem difficult to obtain. But I have to tell you, there is no room for cowardice in this world. If you fear everything and buckle when the smallest pressure or trial comes against you, you're not going to succeed at much.

So how can you acquire courage if you don't have it and you're always afraid?

You take small steps, slowly building success upon success. Each victory will give you more courage to face new challenges and unknown situations.

People have tendencies to remain with what's familiar, in their own false-sense-of-security serenity bubbles, even if it makes them miserable. They're afraid of the unknown because—well, because it's unknown, and they're hesitant to try anything new that might cause them to fail.

So the first thing you have to get into your mind is not to be afraid of failing. Because even if you do, there will always be other doors ready to open for you. Really. There's always something else. Failure isn't the end of your world, and you have to believe that.

Many in the Middle East find this Western concept hard to accept and embrace. There isn't much forgiveness in Arab societies whether you're talking about longstanding family feuds or failures in business. I've found the farther east you travel in the world, the less forgiving societies are and the more strongly ingrained is the sense of saving face—the concept of not being embarrassed, looking foolish, or admitting you failed or you're wrong. Some cultures even believe it's better to commit suicide rather than lose face. The result is individuals in those cultures take fewer risks because they can't accept that they might fail. Which means they don't succeed at much either. They're just stuck in safe, nonchallenging positions.

I don't agree with that.

You have to step out of that shell of your existence and take chances. Fear of the unknown or failure can paralyze you, and that means you won't try anything new. You can't be afraid to fail at something. You're human. You're going to fail. Now use that to grow stronger. Don't be so stuck on the idea that you have to be perfect at everything. If your failure hurts someone, apologize, try to fix it as much as possible, and move on. Don't allow it to paralyze you, and don't let fear get a good foothold.

The ancient Greek philosopher Aristotle said the best way to avoid criticism is to say nothing, do nothing, and be nothing. Are you going to let your fear of criticism keep you from accomplishing anything?

It may sound odd, but one of the best ways to get over a fear of failure is to pick a new activity or sport and deliberately decide to fail at it—just so you can try the experience without any pressure on you. Take up golf, learn chess, study a new language. Don't go into it with any expectations other than to have fun. You may be surprised by how well you do. And you may find you really enjoy learning new things. You don't have to do *everything* well. You just have to get in the habit of not being afraid to experience new opportunities.

Once you realize failing at something isn't the end of the world, you won't be afraid to try more new things. And with each new attempt at conquering the unknown, you'll gain successes and more courage to face whatever challenges lie ahead of you. You'll also shed just a little more of that detrimental fear.

Another thing to remember is that most events we're afraid of never happen. It's easy to create in our minds entire lists of possible doomsday scenarios that could prevent us from moving forward. But realize there's a very good chance most of the things you're afraid will happen never will. You're worrying and becoming fearful over nothing.

The important thing is for you not to be afraid of trying something new, whether it's going an unfamiliar place, changing jobs, or even moving to a new country. If you're still afraid to take the first step, then pick a small new activity and do it spontaneously—spur of the moment, without thinking about it too much. Set goals, and don't be afraid to go forward pursuing them no matter how far out of your comfort zone you have to step.

Of course in order to achieve success, you always need to prepare yourself adequately before you attempt something major and life changing. You can't just jump in without doing your homework. You need to educate yourself, look at all the things that could go wrong, and make preparations to conquer or skirt those obstacles. Being well prepared can give you a certain sense of security when you're dealing with the unknown.

Another thing to consider is that being different or standing out from the crowd isn't a bad thing. Don't be afraid to be different. What you're attempting may not be what everyone else is doing, but maybe that's because you're on the cutting edge of new ideas or technology.

It may help you to find someone who supports you as you step into the unknown and try new things. Having support can boost your confidence and calm your nerves. Hopefully it's a close family member, but some people aren't always that fortunate. You may need to find a mentor or friend who cheers you on and encourages you to take the chances you need to achieve victory. Keep searching until you find that support.

Everyone needs moral strength—the ability to stand up for his or her beliefs without being afraid. Even if people criticize you, and your peers try to persuade you to do otherwise, remain steadfast in what you know is right. Too many people are so weak minded, they allow others to influence their actions and even their thoughts. I encourage you to stop worrying about what others think of you or your actions. Be brave, and courageously follow your heart, taking the actions you know to be right and true even if others don't support you or are too afraid to step forward with you. You may find in a short while that once you start achieving success with your actions, the same people criticizing you will start following you.

Become courageous and strong.

How I Gained Courage and Strength

I learned from a very early age that I needed strength and courage—especially after my young, carefree, innocent life in the Middle East ended, and cold reality left me a refugee.

World Wars I and II drastically altered Palestine, where I spent my early years. The armistice of November 11, 1918, ended the First World War—the "Great War" that, unrealistically, was supposed to end all wars—with the United States, Great Britain, and their allies emerging as the victors. The Turks, who for six hundred years had ruled the Ottoman Empire including much of the Middle East, were defeated, having sided with the Germans and the Central Powers.

The Arabs, who had grown to loathe the Turks, had joined Britain and the rest of the Allied Powers and received encouragement to unite as brothers. The idea of Arab unity has been around for more than 1,400 years—since the AD 600s, when the prophet Mohammad (peace be upon him) attempted it with religion.

When I attended college at American University of Beirut, I enjoyed reading the works of Lebanese Maronite Christian writers who advocated Arab nationalism—writers such as Dr. Philip Khuri Hitti, a professor who taught at AUB and Princeton University in New Jersey, and Butrus Al-Bustani, an Arab Protestant who helped translate the Bible into Arabic from the original Greek, Hebrew, and Aramaic. Those writers made me think Arab unity might be possible if it were along secular lines, not incorporating Islam.

During World War I, the charismatic British duo of T. E. "Lawrence of Arabia" Lawrence and Gertrude Bell was particularly supportive of Arab unity. After the war they continued to give input to politicians and greatly contributed to the carving up of the Middle East when the boundary lines of the modern-day nations began to be drawn. Britain retained civil administrative rule in Palestine from 1920 to 1948, and the area became known as the British Mandate of Palestine.

Jews fleeing Eastern European pogroms had been pouring into Palestine since the 1880s, but in November 1917 the actions of British Foreign Secretary Arthur Balfour, a Scot who'd formerly been Britain's prime minister, seemed to encourage even more Jewish immigration. Balfour wrote a letter to Baron Walter Rothshield stating the British government wanted to establish Palestine as a national home for Jews. However, Balfour stipulated in the letter that Arabs' civil and religious rights in Palestine weren't to be affected.

The floodgates to Jewish immigration opened wide in the lead-up to World War II. German chancellor Adolf Hitler's actions and those of his Nazi party in the 1930s led more than 250,000 Jews to flee Europe and immigrate to Palestine, an action that caused massive unemployment for Arabs, infuriating them. It was life changing for many, including my family.

That was the world I entered on October 13, 1930.

I was born in Nablus, Palestine, the hometown of my mother, Mahdiyyeh—a city located about thirty-five miles north of Jerusalem in what's now the Palestinian-controlled West Bank. But I spent the first thirteen years of my life in the ancient port city of Jaffa along the shore of the Mediterranean Sea. About 90 percent of Jaffa's residents were Arabs (the area is still predominantly Arab). Tel Aviv absorbed Jaffa into its municipal limits in 1950, its rapid growth due mainly to decades of Jewish immigration.

My father, Taleb, followed in the profession of many in his family and was a merchant in Jaffa. He'd courageously started his own money-changing business at the age of seventeen, when the end of World War I left Palestine's currency very fluid. Two years later he'd seamlessly moved into his own wholesale business, importing rice, sugar, and coffee.

I was extremely fortunate to have the family life I did while growing up. My father was my earliest inspiration for becoming an entrepreneur. From the time I was five, when I started a little candy-apple business, to the formation of my international corporation, Hikma, I've always tried to emulate my father's wonderful example of self-discipline, industriousness, and hard work as he fearlessly tried new things.

My peaceful life in Jaffa and British-controlled Palestine soon came to an end. Arabs were fed up with the massive number of Jews immigrating into Palestine. They were also sick of the British. On April 15, 1936, Arabs shot and killed two Jewish truck drivers traveling in a convoy on the road linking Nablus to Tulkarem. The next day the Jews retaliated, killing two Arabs. Tensions between the two groups escalated over the next few days, resulting in the deaths of twenty-two people and wounding more than one hundred others. Arabs closed all their shops in Jaffa in a general protest against the Jews and the British.

My father closed his shop, but the goods he'd already ordered continued to arrive, forcing him to rent warehouse space to store his ever-growing (and nonselling) inventory. With no money coming in, my parents, my brother, my sister, and I struggled to survive. Three months later, as tensions mounted in Jaffa and with fighting all around us, my father decided we should move to Nablus and live with my grandparents—a risky journey because my mother was seven months pregnant with her fourth child.

Eventually, after traveling by train, on foot, and even in a horse-drawn cart, we made it safely to my grandparents' home. It was quite an experience for a five-year-old, an early lesson in survival that definitely strengthened me.

We returned to our home in Jaffa three months later, but almost immediately the Arab Revolt began, spurred on by Arab anger at British rule as well as the continuing influx of Jewish immigrants. The uprising lasted three years, resulting in a lot of bloodshed for Arabs, Jews, and the British. It ended only when the British released a white paper that recommended giving Arabs more civil rights and limiting the number of Jewish immigrants. It didn't help much. Tensions continued to rise, and, shortly after the Arab Revolt ended, World War II began. The white paper was set aside, martial law was declared, and blackouts became mandatory. Food was scarce.

Because sea transport was so dangerous during World War II, large ships weren't delivering goods at the port in Jaffa, which was disastrous for some merchants. But my father was extremely resourceful and bought a small boat to pick up his supplies at Port Said in Egypt, where the large ships docked, then he sailed them back to Jaffa. Because of that my father's business remained quite lucrative. He sank his profits into real estate and some of the orange orchards for which Jaffa was famous as well as two citrus groves in Tulkarem.

The war was stressful, with bombers frequently flying over, but there was also an air of excitement mixed in with the danger. I had a loving, happy home, and for a child that's the most important thing. My family's been my constant over the years, and they've sustained me through some pretty horrendous times. Besides that, children are pretty resilient—even during war.

But at thirteen, right at the height of the war, I had to acquire a healthy dose of courage. I was offered a scholarship to attend the Arab College in Jerusalem, which meant I had to leave my family. Both of my parents strongly supported education, and even in the middle of the war they wanted me to keep learning. I loved school and was excited about traveling to a new city, but the moment my older brother dropped me off and left to return to Jaffa, a wave of loneliness and fear overwhelmed me.

I'm sure many children who have been sent off to boarding schools around the world have felt the same despair the first time they were left alone without their support systems. You're forced to grow up in a hurry. There are no more hugs and kisses when you go to bed at night, no parents or siblings there to help calm you when you're upset. It's a difficult situation for a child. Many college-age students go through the same separation anxiety. The first time you're forced to live away from home, it changes you. I cried, realizing I was totally alone in a strange new city—a difficult situation for a young boy. But I wanted my parents to be proud of me, so I forced myself to get over my fears, and with that mental strength I gained a bit more courage. Eventually I fell in love with all my classes, the other students, and the instructors at the school, but it wasn't easy reaching that point. I was in a situation where I was forced to be brave and acquire courage.

I was still in school when the war ended in 1945. Jews and Arabs were still fighting each other as Jewish immigrants from Europe continued to pour into Palestine. Both groups wanted the British out of Palestine, so they attacked them too. All three groups had grown to hate each other, and the blood flowed.

I graduated in 1947, the same year the British became totally fed up with the Arabs' and Jews' conflict and decided to kick the matter to the United Nations. The UN voted on November 29 to partition Palestine into two states, one Jewish and one Arab. The Jews accepted it; the Arabs didn't. The British accepted the decision but refused to implement it. Instead they pretty much stopped governing the country and started making plans to leave.

The body count mounted as the Jews, Arabs, and British continued attacking each other. In a two-month period, almost one thousand were killed, and more than 1,100 were wounded.

Then the fighting came to my town. On January 4, 1948, Jewish terrorists, in broad daylight, drove a car loaded with explosives into the center of Jaffa and detonated it next to the building that housed the town council and the headquarters of the Arab National Committee, killing ten and injuring scores more. Within days Arabs had retaliated against Jewish communities in Northern Palestine and pinned Jews inside Jerusalem's Old City, a blockade that lasted for five months.

My country was filled with hate and in shambles. We all struggled not to let fear overwhelm us, but we were terrified.

Three months later, on April 25, the Jews' Irgun and Haganah began bombing Jaffa. We knew if we didn't leave our home, there was a strong chance we'd all be killed. My parents, my three brothers, my three sisters, and I packed up the few belongings we could carry and fled, refugees in the midst of war. We didn't have much cash. My father had sunk all his profits into real estate, but because of the conflict that was worth less than what he'd paid for it.

As gunfire whizzed over our heads, my family fled toward Nablus, where we had relatives, but there was no space for us. Finally we found a few small rooms where the nine of us would live for a few months. Three weeks after we'd fled, however, the Arabs who had remained in Jaffa surrendered to the Jews. The next day, May 14, the British packed up, turned over Palestine to the UN, and left the country. The Arabs and Jews immediately unleashed more violence on each other. The Jews declared Palestine a Jewish state named Israel; the Arab League called for a jihad—a holy war—against the Jews; and the armies of Egypt, Syria, Transjordan, Lebanon, and Iraq invaded Palestine from all sides.

I grieved for the loss not only of my home, my city, and my country but also my future. I was totally frustrated because I couldn't attend college or find a job. My life was on hold, a year of it totally wasted. My father tried to reestablish his business in Nablus, but it wasn't successful at all. Even then he stressed that no matter how hopeless our situation seemed, even in the midst of war, we were still responsible for our actions and had to try to improve ourselves and our circumstances.

I'm sure many people today can relate to what I was going through then. With the massive unemployment around the world today as well as housing foreclosures and multiple wars that have created refugees, they know what it's like to not have homes, money, jobs, or even countries. Being in that kind of situation can leave you feeling hopeless and helpless, but I urge those who are not to give up. Eventually things will turn around. Sometimes events cause one to sink to a low point, but in time everything improves. That's the cycle of life.

Eventually my father found work in Amman, the capital of

what was then called Transjordan (which in 1951 was renamed the Hashemite Kingdom of Jordan), and our family moved to be with him. Like many refugees of war, we were thankful a new country was willing to take us in and allow us to begin life anew. My family is living proof that even if you're penniless, homeless, and without a country, you can still once again create a good life—in many cases an even better life than you had before. You just need to have the courage and strength to go forward, to keep trying to succeed, and not to become overwhelmed by despair.

For thousands of years, wars have created refugees who have been forced to relocate to new nations, many times with only the clothes on their backs. It's one of the most traumatic experiences a person can go through. But it's not the end of the world if one keeps the proper mental attitude.

When we first moved to Amman, we were cold and hungry. Our apartment had no central heat, only a stove for warmth, and we had very little money. We mourned the loss of our previous life in our wonderful home surrounded by the orange groves of Jaffa. But when my father was able to reestablish his business in Transjordan, our financial situation slowly improved. My father's courage in bravely moving forward with his life taught us all to be strong.

A few months after my family had settled in Amman, somehow representatives from the American University of Beirut found me. They were traveling through the Middle East interviewing prospective students, and they invited me to attend their school. It's true: chance and circumstance can play large parts in your success.

AUB, one of the top-rated colleges in the world, was founded in 1866. It was the first American university in a foreign country, and each student's degree was registered with the New York Board of Regents. The school placed an emphasis on medical-related fields and collaborated with noted American universities such as Johns Hopkins in Baltimore, George Washington University in Washington, DC, and Columbia University in New York as well as international schools such as the University of Paris.

For me it was a dream come true.

By then my father's business was doing well, and he could afford to pay my tuition, so in October 1949 I moved to Beirut, Lebanon. Again I had to work up the courage to leave my close, loving family and travel all by myself to a new country.

Even though I was an excellent student for the first two years at AUB, toward the end of my second year I met a beautiful girl named Samira. As my third school year began, I found myself falling deeper in love with her. I thought about her constantly and tried to spend as much time as possible with her, ignoring my studies. My grades plunged, causing me to fail my junior year. It was humiliating, especially because I was anxious to finish school and marry Samira, but I swallowed my pride and repeated my third year of college, this time maintaining a high grade-point average. The experience taught me a lot. As I have said, failure isn't fatal. Sometimes you can learn more from the experience of failing than you would if you'd been perfect all along.

Samira and I married, but when I graduated in 1954 I couldn't find a job in my field. My bachelor's of science degree was in pharmacy, and I'd thought it would solve all my problems. It didn't. Eventually I found a job teaching science in Lebanon. It wasn't what I wanted, but at least it paid the bills.

A year later I finally landed my first job as a pharmacist at a hospital in Kuwait. But after three years, I realized I was bored out of my mind with dispensing drugs all day. By then Samira and I had three children; we were doing well financially, but I knew I needed more of a challenge. After examining the possibilities and discussing my options with Samira, I finally decided to step out on faith and quit my well-paying job. We moved back to Amman, and I bought a pharmacy.

Because I knew how uncertain life could be, I started teaching my children how to be strong and courageous, to be prepared for when things didn't work out, how to survive without me, how to make wise decisions on their own, and to be independent. I knew if their lives were going to be anything like mine, one day they would need those skills to make their ways in the world.

Within a few years, I'd mastered the skill of owning a store, and it had become successful. But again I discovered I was bored with being a pharmacist. My life had become too predictable, and I craved new challenges.

I'd read in a newspaper that the US State Department was accepting applications for foreign students to receive Fulbright grants to attend college in America. Because the American University of Beirut was a US-based university, when I'd been a student there we'd studied the history, culture, and government of the United States. I had been fascinated and had decided I wanted to live there one day.

It was a wonderful dream, but in reality I was a thirty-two-year-old married father of four, with my children ranging in age from three to ten. Still, my wonderful, understanding wife urged me to apply for a Fulbright grant just to see if they'd select me. They did. Samira encouraged me to accept the opportunity, giving me her stamp of approval. She said we'd work it out somehow.

I arranged for my brother and a friend to run my pharmacy, then Samira, our children, and I packed our bags for the United States. Once again I had to dig down for the courage to leave everything familiar and move halfway around the world to attend postgraduate school at the St. Louis College of Pharmacy in Missouri. A year later, as I prepared to graduate with a master's in industrial pharmacy, some of the largest and most prestigious pharmaceutical companies in the world started recruiting me, including Eli Lilly, Abbott, and Upjohn. I decided Eli Lilly was the right fit for me and offered the best opportunities for my future.

For the next twelve years, I not only moved up through the corporate ranks of Eli Lilly but also physically moved around the world: from Richmond, Virginia, to Indianapolis, Indiana, to Beirut, Lebanon, to London, to Rome, and back to Beirut. I never could have done that if I'd let fear rule my life. Instead I viewed each move as another great chance to learn about a culture and meet new people.

Courage will open your life to wonderful opportunities.

When war broke out in Lebanon in April 1975, only weeks

after Eli Lilly had relocated me there to set up our regional operations, I was forced to return to Rome. The fighting I witnessed was traumatic for me and brought back memories of the war during my childhood, but courage builds upon courage. Whatever you've gained in prior experiences helps you face the next tougher battle. The more you have to step up, the stronger you become.

Even though I had a great job in management at Eli Lilly, was making a top salary, and loved our life in Rome, Samira and I still felt like refugees with no country to call our own. We were afraid our children were going to grow up without any kind of national identity or home base. Samira's family had left Palestine because of the fighting around the same time as my family. We'd gone to Amman while her family had chosen Lebanon. Now both of us wanted a place to call home. We wanted something permanent.

Being without a country of my own for so many years had taught me a lot of great lessons. I'd learned to adapt to different cultures, something that was useful in building a successful international business. I'd also seen the influence local and cultural traditions have on a company's satellite offices.

I had a secure job at Eli Lilly, but when you work for someone else the fact is you're dispensable and can be replaced at any time. On top of that, even though I'd risen through the ranks of the company, I'd lived in so many different places, I always felt my homes were temporary. I knew owning my own business was very risky, but at least I would be my own boss, and that meant I could finally settle in to some form of permanence. So in 1976 I made the risky decision to leave my steady job and regular paycheck to take a dive into the void and insecurity of starting my own pharmaceutical company in Amman, Jordan.

Building a new business is all about making careful calculations then courageously taking risks. The Western world has many examples of successful corporations, but I was starting my company in the Middle East, which was a huge gamble. There aren't many Arab models of entrepreneurship. One reason is governments set regulations for businesses and, in a politically unstable environment such as the Middle East, where governments and their regulations change frequently, new companies may not financially be able to make the changes required of them.

Generally the higher the social standard of a country, the better and more affordable hospitals and medical care become. People in Jordan, my adopted country, have health care, and there is government assistance for the poor. It's always good if more of a country's budget is allocated to health services, but unfortunately, usually the first thing new governments in MENA countries do to cut the national budget is lower prices for pharmaceuticals. Companies have to comply or get out of the market.

One trait successful entrepreneurs and many refugees have is optimism. They believe things will work out well in the future, and that sustains them through the difficult times. I know it sustained me. More than anything I've had to have courage and mental fortitude even when things were falling apart.

You need to be brave and strong if you're going to survive in this world—and definitely if you're planning to oversee a global enterprise.

LESSON TWO

Keep Learning

It was another beautiful day in Amman, but my frustration wasn't allowing me to enjoy it as much as I would have liked. As I sat in a directors' meeting at the Jubilee School, listening to the chairman of the board tell us of yet another student who was rejecting our scholarship offer, an idea that had been brewing in my mind for a while began to come together more completely.

Like many corporate executives around the world, I'm often invited to give my input and serve on the boards of directors for various organizations in addition to my own company's. Though I'm honored whenever I'm asked, unfortunately I simply don't have the time to agree to each outside position. But there are some offers that inspire me so much, I have to accept.

One board I'd enthusiastically wanted to be part of was for the Jubilee School for Gifted and Talented Students in Amman, a project the late King Hussein and his wife, Queen Noor, strong proponents of education, had first envisioned in 1977—the year of the king's Silver Jubilee as ruler of Jordan.

Queen Noor knew I shared the king's passion for education and asked me to join the Jubilee School's board in 1991, two years before it officially opened in a temporary building. The school, which now boasts an enrollment of 350 students in grades nine through twelve, is noted for its program designed specifically for gifted students, particularly those from underprivileged families who can't afford to pay for quality education. Jubilee fills a critical need because if gifted students aren't given the proper mental challenges through education, they stand the risk of becoming bored with education—a dangerous scenario. Their minds are hungry for knowledge, with voracious appetites to learn more and more, and teachers need to be there for them to fulfill those needs.

What many don't realize is gifted students, if not properly challenged, suffer a disproportionately high dropout rate. Such brilliant minds are wasted if they're not properly directed. Students are a nation's future, and all of them need to be nurtured carefully, including the gifted, who can contribute so much.

The Jubilee School's goals are everything in which my family and I believed. Not only had my parents insisted my brothers, my sisters, and I got good educations, but my wife and I had both been teachers. My wife, Samira, had taught school in Lebanon, Kuwait, and Jordan then moved into administration, becoming a school supervisor for the United Nations Relief and Works Agency for Palestine Refugees in the Near East (UNRWA). I'd been a teacher before beginning my pharmaceutical career.

That was why I felt so frustrated during the board meeting at the Jubilee School on that day in 2006. As the chairman of the board delivered his report, we learned once again that the parents of a girl from Southern Jordan possessing a brilliant mind and holding such great promise had vetoed the idea of her coming to Amman to enroll in our school. They didn't want their young daughter living so far away in a boarding school no matter how wonderful the opportunity might have been. Students from Amman and the regions surrounding it almost always accepted our offers and attended the school. But because the southern region was so far away and so remote, families from there rarely responded positively to our recruitment—especially the parents of girls.

The southern part of the Hashemite Kingdom, which shares a border with Saudi Arabia, is home to most of Jordan's natural resources, in particular our phosphate mines. We're one of the largest exporters of phosphate in the world, with the high-grade Ash Shidiyah mine holding an estimated one billion tons of the mineral. The southern region also boasts marble, shale-oil rocks, silica, and copper deposits.

Ideally, because of those resources, many industries should be located in the south—but only a few are. And mainly that's because Jordanians living there haven't had as much education as those in the northern parts of the country near the capital, Amman. Even though Jordan has one of the most educated populations in the Middle East and places a strong emphasis on education for both boys and girls, with a national literacy rate of more than 92 percent, there aren't many schools in the Southern area, particularly for girls.

One of the reasons I'd selected Jordan as my new homeland so many years before was women were given more opportunities there both in education and careers—more than in most places in the Middle East. Sad to say, but some parts of the Arab world are stuck in the Dark Ages when it comes to equal opportunities for women. I think part of it is the men know how smart women are and are afraid their egos will be bruised if they compete on an equal field.

It was a passion for education, especially for girls, that led my wife and me to select Jordan as our permanent country. We wanted our two daughters to grow up knowing they could achieve anything they wanted to—with enough hard work and perseverance. We didn't want anything to hold them back from achieving the same successes as their brothers. Our sons and daughters grew up knowing how powerful women can be.

The main reason to make the education of girls a national priority is, ultimately, it leads to a better nation. No matter what country you're in, whether you're male or female, usually the first person who educates you and starts setting your standards is your mother or a female nanny.

It saddened me to think the potential of young girls from the southern region of Jordan might be wasted simply because they didn't have access to good education. I knew from personal experience how difficult, frightening, and lonely it can be to go to boarding school at that age. My parents had insisted I attend the Arab School in Jerusalem when I was offered a scholarship. Not only was I boarding away from home all by myself, but it was the middle of World War II—two frightening events. Decades later a few of my children would go through the same experience of attending a boarding school in the middle of a war zone.

What I'd been considering for a while was this: if parents from the South wouldn't allow their daughters to come to our school in Amman, then school was simply going to have to go to them. I contacted Jordan's Ministry of Education to ask the officials there if I could fund a school for them. They enthusiastically welcomed my offer and told me there was no school for girls in Al Shobak, a village approximately 130 miles south of Amman and fewer than twenty miles north of the famed ancient city of Petra, one of Jordan's main tourist attractions. The area around Shobak is mainly agricultural and is blessed with not only fertile land where farmers grow grains, figs, olives, and grapes but also abundant springs to water those crops.

Unfortunately they hadn't been blessed with a school for girls.

The Ministry of Education provided a rough suggestion for the design of the building then offered to give me a plot of land located on a hill overlooking the center of town. My architects and construction crews began work on the US$1 million building, and eighteen months later Jordan's King Abdullah II cut the ribbon at the front door, officially opening the Samih Darwazah School for Girls. (Jordanian law requires a school building be named after the person paying for it.)

Samira and I were ecstatic and emotional as we stood there with tears in our eyes watching the ceremony, feeling as if we'd just personally given birth to hundreds of new, brilliant daughters. As many as five hundred primary- and middle-school-aged girls up to grade ten now had a place where they could thrive, grow, and nurture dreams for their futures.

In June 2013 five students from our school teamed up with American students from Elm Place Middle School near Chicago, Illinois, and made international headlines. The team competed at the Future Problem Solving Program International Conference at Indiana University in Bloomington. The Jordanian-and-American team went on to win first place for having the best and most creative project for their division. Their Operation Tefkiir

(*tefkiir* means "think" in Arabic) focused not only on teaching critical and creative thinking skills but also on abolishing stereotypes. To do that the students had a cultural book exchange. Our students sent books to the Americans that demonstrated some of our Jordanian customs, and the Americans sent books to our students to translate and read to younger ones at the school.

The combined team also won the competition's highest honor—The Beyonder Award, given to students with a project so far beyond the others it's not even on the same scale.

Our Jordanian students were the only ones from an Arab country to participate in the competition. We are so proud of them and all our students.

Two years after our school opened in Al Shobak, May, Said, Mazen, and Hana followed in my footsteps, giving an endowment to Samira's and my alma mater, American University of Beirut, to establish a research center at its Olayyan School of Business. Both AUB's president and the dean of the business school delivered my children's present to me via phone call on October 13, 2010—my eightieth birthday—and it was one of the best gifts I've ever received.

The Samih Darwazah Center for Innovative Management and Entrepreneurship officially opened three months later, on January 14, 2011. The business center, which combines the best practices from the Middle East and the West, allows graduate students working on their MBAs to deal with real-life case studies in the Arab world. The students then have their results published in order to allow others to learn from them and improve business across the region. It's inspiring to think how much something like that not only benefits future generations of Middle Eastern entrepreneurs but tears down geographical and cultural boundaries.

The center's main office has a beautiful view of the Mediterranean Sea, with one large room for school executives and assistants and another room containing laptops and workstations for graduate students. Two full-time employees from the university and six or seven students organize lectures, set up internships, and keep records.

Three or four days before the center's opening ceremony, there were political concerns in Beirut (which wasn't particularly surprising—welcome to Lebanon), but my risk-taking family and friends showed up anyway. That's how much we love education.

Besides being courageous and strong, you need to receive a proper education to achieve not only your short-term goals but also your long-term ones. Becoming a successful global entrepreneur involves continuous learning. Education is the one thing of value you always carry with you no matter where you live. It's portable. That's something refugees know all too well. My parents had taught me homes, businesses, property, and possessions could all be taken away from me without a moment's notice, but no one could take the education in my mind and the dreams stemming from that.

I had been fortunate enough to receive a scholarship to attend the Arab College in Jerusalem when I was young, and as Palestinian refugees Samira and I both had received help in obtaining higher education. Because of that we wanted to help other Palestinian refugees and selected Birzeit University, located near Ramallah, Palestine, through which to do so.

Birzeit was established in 1924, the first institution of higher education in Palestine. It began as a girls' elementary school then expanded to include a separate boys' school, then a high school and eventually a university. The school awarded its first bachelor's degrees in 1976. Today it offers forty-seven bachelor's programs and twenty-six master's. The student body has grown from 239 in 1972 to more than ten thousand students today (nearly 8,500 undergraduates and more than one thousand graduate students), and the campus now has twenty-four main buildings—quite a change from the single building where it began almost one hundred years ago. Approximately two-thirds of the students are young women, which greatly pleases me.

Samira and I decided the best way we could help Birzeit University and its students would be to donate funds to build and furnish a pharmacy facility there. It should be completed within the next year. Currently I serve on the university's board of directors, which provides an even better opportunity for me to help the students. Birzeit University also recently honored me when they told me they'd selected me to receive an honorary doctorate.

Samira, ever the teacher, then went on to establish a nursing scholarship at the American University of Beirut. The Samira Fadli Scholarship is earmarked for young Palestinian women who are orphans. After the recipients graduate, most usually find lucrative jobs in the medical field—a boost up in life for those who started out with nothing. Not only that but nursing, like most medical skills, is always needed to help people living in the West Bank and Gaza Strip. The scholarship is awarded consecutively: when the current holder of the award graduates, it's then awarded to another student.

Samira and I also established a scholarship at Lebanese American University, the school where our son, Mazen, and some of our grandchildren obtained their bachelor's degrees. This scholarship is awarded to a Jordanian or Palestinian student specializing in pharmaceutical studies. Of course it goes without saying that students have to maintain excellent grades in order to qualify and keep both scholarships.

A University Degree Is Mandatory, Not Optional

As my parents stressed to me, and as my wife and I made clear to our four children, graduating from high school and college is mandatory. Why? Well, one reason is pure economics. If you have a college degree, you're more likely to be employed than if you don't have one. You'll also have a better paycheck. On average, if you graduate with a bachelor's degree, you can earn at least 60 percent more than if you have only a high-school diploma. If you have a master's degree, on average you'll have double the salary you would if you'd never gone to college. And if you continue on to get your doctorate degree, you can earn more than three times as much than if you'd settled for only a high-school diploma. In this day of fast-changing technology and needs, you may even find you have to continue your education with postgraduate work or change careers completely because your bachelor's degree, and the career associated with it, is no longer enough to guarantee you a job. For those who say college is too expensive and not an option, I say do your research. Besides countries around the world regularly providing financial assistance to their young citizens both in their homelands and abroad, there are also hundreds of thousands of scholarships and fellowships available. That's *free money*. And here's the thing many people don't realize: a lot of those scholarships go unawarded each year because no one applies for them. You have to take your time and dig for them, and probably spend some time on the Internet searching, but it's worth it. Corporations, governments, small and large special-interest groups, universities—they all offer scholarships and fellowships.

Many scholarship committees require applicants to provide copies of their grades as well as essays and letters of recommendation, but again it's *free money* for a college education. You just have to take the time to apply—not a difficult task if someone's going to be handing you a check.

As a last resort, many countries also provide student loans that don't have to be repaid until after graduation.

High school and college degrees are only the beginning—the basic foundation upon which to continue to build your skills. If you don't realize that, you'll be settling for the mediocre. Continuing your education, and not necessarily in a formal classroom, is the difference between being content with maintaining the status quo and having a successful and productive career.

You must always keep learning—and you must always give your hand to others to help them learn too.

Employee Education

My family and I are strong proponents of obtaining both under-graduate and graduate degrees from the best university you can afford. Samira's and my love of education comes partially from our backgrounds. In Palestine, where our families were from, education was always the focus. In almost every household, the first money that came in would go toward education. What was left would then be divvied up for food and clothing. When we were forced to flee our homes and our country, we could carry only limited amounts of food and clothing, but our educations helped us survive wherever we ended up.

Samira and I always tried to set the example that men and women are equal. We both received our undergraduate degrees from American University of Beirut. My wife graduated first, in June 1951, with a bachelor of arts degree in political science and history; then, after we married in October 1952, she taught school and helped financially support me for more than a year until I graduated with a bachelor of science in pharmacy in June 1954. As I mentioned earlier, I went on to get my master's on a Fulbright scholarship.

Samira and I wanted our four children to have at least the same educational opportunities we'd had—and even to go beyond that if they wanted. But all four knew it wasn't a matter of *if* they went to college. It was understood they would at least get their undergraduate degrees. And all four did.

At Hikma education isn't just a philosophy—it's our policy. I've always encouraged my employees, whether family or not, to pursue higher education. That's because I know if they expand their thinking and keep learning, they'll not only move up more quickly through the company but also do well in any position to which we assign them. To make that possible, Hikma always picks up all expenses for our management personnel's continuing education whether they're taking intensive short-term courses or completing degrees.

A young man named Ibrahim Shihadeh came to me one day in 1978—Hikma's first operational year. He'd just graduated from a technical high school and was looking for a job but seemed very apologetic about not having an extensive résumé.

"I don't have any experience," he said humbly.

"Are you able to learn?" I asked.

He thought I was kidding, but when he realized I wasn't, he said of course he was able to learn. He started at Hikma as a technician, but I encouraged him to go further with his education and offered to pay his tuition. Within ten years he'd completed an advanced degree in physics at Jordan University. Whatever Hikma paid for his college expenses we more than made back in increased productivity. Ibrahim helped double our output and expand our product line and eventually became general manager of our plant in Algeria.

Another young man came to me shortly after he'd finished high school. Khader Jarwan was eager to work but hadn't attended any college classes. I saw a lot of potential in him. He started as a production technician at Hikma and did well, receiving numerous promotions—first to warehouse manager then shipping and exports manager and finally sales-operations manager. He was a diamond who just needed a little more polishing, so one day I pulled him aside and suggested he think about finally pursuing a college education. He agreed but was stunned by the direction I wanted him to go. I suggested he get his bachelor's degree in finance—a field of study far removed from his technical experience.

He wasn't sure if he had it in him, but he worked hard and was one of the happiest men I'd ever seen on the day of his graduation. But just as I'd done with my children, I pushed some more, this time suggesting he continue his formal education and get his master's degree, which he did. All told, Khader took more than one hundred college courses, all of which Hikma paid for. Was it worth it? We thought so. He also became general manager of our Algerian facility.

Hikma's policy is to send almost all our top management to a six-week executive-training program at INSEAD in France. It's not cheap. The course can easily cost US$40,000 per person, but it's worth every cent and has always been a good return on our investment. Hikma has benefitted by gaining more knowledgeable employees who then provide better output.

Because INSEAD is so world renowned, many of the world's

top corporations send their employees there for further education. But that kind of Fortune 500 star power can be a little intimidating at times. Years ago, when we were still relatively new and our profits were small, our corporate vice president of active pharmaceutical ingredients (API), Fadi Nassar, was attending INSEAD for the executive-training course. As expected he found himself surrounded by employees of multibillion-dollar corporations such as Sony and Johnson & Johnson. As if that weren't intimidating enough, they started getting nosy, asking him for Hikma's numbers.

"What are the annual sales of your company?" one of them asked Fadi.

"About a hundred and fifty million dollars," he said.

That's peanuts to the megacorporations, but instead of turning up his nose, the man was impressed.

"You're very lucky to be here," he said. "Most companies that size don't put such a premium on their employees' educations."

That's probably why they don't grow.

During the course Fadi had to prepare a few PowerPoint presentations, which he created himself, along with some flashcards. In contrast another attendee, who was from Johnson & Johnson, produced three very professional-looking presentations. His corporation hired consultants to do the project for him. Ah, star power.

After our employees have received training at institutions such as INSEAD or been to other meetings, conferences, or courses, we ask them to come back to Hikma and make presentations to their colleagues to teach them what they've learned. This not only benefits other Hikma employees but is a good way for those fresh out of training to remember what they've just learned. By teaching their coworkers, employees achieve a deeper understanding of the material themselves.

We're all still learning. Hikma employees have to learn new techniques in order to stay on top of industry trends, and some of the best training can be done on the job, working side by side with a manager. Most people retain much more by first observing then listening and finally attempting the job themselves rather than simply being told how the job is done. That's because people remember 10 percent of what they hear, 30 percent of what they see and hear, and almost 100 percent of what they see, hear, and do. Besides sending our employees to schools and conferences for additional training, we also conduct our own in-house courses to teach our younger workers about corporate management. Othman Abu Ghedia, our corporate human-resources director, became a trainer the second year he was with our company because we quickly realized he's the perfect mentor to teach others management skills. That's because he's positive, fair, and bold, and not at all afraid to say what he thinks—a trait he picked up from his years of study in the United States.

Because Hikma is a global company, we like our employees to get diverse educations from different geographical and philosophical views. We span the globe, and their thinking should too.

Khalid Nabilsi, our current CFO, is a good example of that. Khalid obtained his bachelor's degree from the University of Jordan, became a certified public accountant in the United States, then went on to get his MBA from the University of Hull in Britain. That kind of diverse education is what makes him so valuable to Hikma when dealing with manufacturing facilities on numerous continents. The CPA degree allowed him to get an understanding of American financials and to link the practical with theory—an important skill in not only investment banking but also advisory capital, where the focus is on multiple projects and is not always guaranteed. The MBA gave him broader knowledge about different aspects of European business and finance, which allowed him to find his specific strengths. That's why we encourage our employees to continue their higher educations. Why stop learning after only four years?

Hikma also covers some costs of education for our employees' children. Every working mother in the company gets financial support to help send her children to kindergarten. We also give out more than fifty scholarships a year to pay high school or university fees and expenses for those who are in financial need.

Not long ago I was with our accounts manager going over an expense sheet. One of the items caught my eye.

"Why do you classify employee education as an expense?" I asked him. "It's an investment, not an expense."

Never stop learning. Education allows individuals to excel. It's good for the employee, even better for the company, and the best possible resource for the future of a country.

Education Is More Than a Classroom

Your university degree will take you only to the first steps of your career. Life will require you add to that—knowledge on top of knowledge. That's because education is more than grades, exams, degrees, or even on-the-job training. It's knowledge you gain from observations of events and people. It's cultural experiences you gain from living in a foreign country. It's the means for you to come up with better, easier, or more productive ways of doing things by reading books and journals, talking to experts, or experimenting on your own.

Some people gain knowledge just by listening and watching others. They observe whether others' actions have positive, victorious outcomes or whether they fail miserably because their processes are flawed and full of mistakes.

Then there are those who can gain knowledge only by enrolling in the school of hard knocks. They have to jump in and experience things personally because they're too impatient to wait to see what the results are when others do them, because they have to micromanage everything, or because they're so untrusting of others they believe their results are the only ones that matter.

Whichever method works best for you, use it. The point is to keep learning every day. You'll never take your company onto the world stage if you don't have a desire to keep learning.

Technology is changing at such a rapid pace, if you refuse to gain more knowledge, you'll be left behind, and so will your company.

Learn from your failures and mistakes and others'. You may need to relearn skills you haven't used in a while or even unlearn something that is detrimental. If you're not already, become a voracious reader. Learn what's going on in the world. Read magazines, books, and especially international newspapers. Tap in to the wealth of knowledge that's available online these days.

Learn how to use a computer, its software, social media, and e-mail. Learn how to do a search online for information. It's mindboggling to me, but there actually are people today who can't master what's now considered basic technology. Even Warren Buffett joined the social media website Twitter—at age eighty-two! On May 2, 2013, his first tweet was, "Warren is in the house." His second tweet was a link to his *Fortune* magazine essay on why women are key to America's prosperity.

Attend experts' lectures or watch them online. You gain wisdom when you can tap in to the brainpower of others. There are many people who are smarter than you are. Don't be defensive about it. Instead learn from them, and add your own creative input to take it to the next level. Stand on their shoulders so you don't waste time learning from scratch everything they already know.

Don't stay closed off and in your own little world. Instead make it a point to be friendly and meet new people everywhere you go: on airplanes or trains, in airports, at restaurants, in elevators. Learn from their life experiences or from the experiences of the people they know. You never know when a chance encounter may give you a fresh perspective, ideas, or contacts that will translate into growth for your company.

Learn from your employees. Learn to read people's body language. It'll help you connect and communicate better with people, and in a business sense it's beneficial when negotiating deals.

Consider auditing university classes as Steve Jobs did—just for the knowledge, not the grades.

The point is you should move from being forced to learn, with your parents and teachers standing over you, to wanting to learn on your own, motivating yourself. Aggressively train yourself to think bigger. Your college degree was useful in starting your career, but the world is moving quickly, and you have to keep learning if you want to keep pace with it, especially if you're going to move ahead and be a frontrunner.

Learn Other Languages

Learning additional languages is something I encourage all executives to continue during their lives. Being able to speak to people who don't come from the same background you do is eye opening, particularly if it's in their native language. One benefit to living in America for a year while I pursued my postdoctorate degree was the chance to master English in the language-immersion lab of real life. English is the second most widely spoken language in the world (only Mandarin Chinese surpasses it) and is the universal language for air traffic controllers and pilots. In 2013 Germany's president, Joachim Gauck, even called for English to become the official language of the multicultural and multilinguistic European Union.

Being able to speak, read, and write fluent English has definitely given me an advantage in life, particularly in business dealings. Knowing the language has also benefited my four children's lives and their business careers. Samira and I were amazed by how easily they all picked up English, especially our youngest, Hana, who was three years old when we moved to Missouri. She was the first in our family to speak English well. After three months in America, all four of our children were fluent. Within six months they'd practically forgotten how to speak Arabic (or at least they pretended not to understand us when we asked them in Arabic to do their chores).

Years later, when Eli Lilly transferred me to Rome, my bosses thought my family and I should learn Italian even though, as an American company, all our business was done in English. The company arranged for one teacher to tutor employees at our office and assigned another teacher to work with our families in our homes.

But Samira, ever the teacher, started instructing her tutor on how to speak her native tongue. After a few days, instead of my wife learning Italian, she had him speaking full sentences in flawless Arabic. Both my wife and I found the skills we learned as teachers carried over into times when neither one of us was officially working in the field of education. I guess we both have a deep desire not only to keep learning but to help others grow mentally too.

While we were living in Rome, Samira, my four children, and I not only learned Italian but mastered it as our third language, and today we still speak it fluently.

You can never know too many languages. With the addition of each one to your skill set, you open doors to an entirely new group of people who speak only that language and with whom you hadn't been able to communicate well before that unless you had a translator. For business dealings, knowing multiple languages is invaluable. You become a great asset to any company where you work.

Learn about Other Cultures

When I was working on my master's degree in St. Louis, churches and schools there would often invite Samira and me to speak about our life in the Middle East. So we obtained films, booklets, and brochures from the Jordanian embassy in Washington, DC, and served as unofficial ambassadors. Some American children's questions could be quite amusing. They would ask whether we rode camels, if we ate with knives and forks, if we lived in tents, and if we knew any famous people from Jordan. We learned a lot about the United States, and hopefully the Americans we spoke to learned a lot about Jordan during our cultural exchange.

My culture in the Middle East had taught me how important

it is not only to belong to a group but also to take care of members of that community as well as your family. I combined that with key business-management rules I learned from my life in the West such as being open minded; listening to others' opinions; adopting and practicing positive thinking; and, most important, always being aware of the results of my actions.

If you ever have the opportunity to live in a foreign country or experience a different culture, you'll have a wonderful learning experience and gain so much extra knowledge you wouldn't if you were just sitting in a classroom. The more exposure you and your children have to different cultures, the better your judgment and the bigger your scope of thinking.

When we were living in Missouri, Samira and I decided to learn as much about the United States as possible. Fortunately we had the money to travel almost every weekend. Each month I received not only a stipend check from the Fulbright Foundation but also the proceeds from my pharmacy in Amman, which my brother sent to me. Samira and I bought a car and took road trips to the Ozark Mountains in Missouri as well as to major cities such as Washington, DC, New York, and Chicago. When the school was on winter break, we explored the Southwest, driving the famous Route 66 from St. Louis to California, stopping in Texas, New Mexico, and Arizona. We learned so much from the people we met while traveling.

When Eli Lilly hired me to be their manager of marketing in the Middle East and moved me there in 1965, the company didn't have much of a presence in the area, so rather than spread myself too thinly through many countries I decided to focus completely on one country at a time before moving on to the next. Each country became an intensive immersion laboratory where I would learn about the culture, the geography, the political climate, and the people, becoming close with many of them. I wanted to know and understand my territory completely. Only then would I line up our marketing representatives and salespeople before finally moving on to the next country. It was definitely a learning experience as I dug deeper into different Arab cultures and their politics.

At times I dealt with the private sector, but in countries such as Syria, where medicine was socialized, I had to maneuver around the red tape of government distributors. Eventually my territory included Lebanon, Jordan, Sudan, Saudi Arabia, Iran, Syria, and Yemen.

In 1971 Eli Lilly transferred me to Rome. Needless to say each restaurant my family and I visited was more delicious than the one before. Since we were in danger of eating ourselves to death, Samira and I enforced a new family rule: nourish your brains before you nourish your stomachs.

We wanted to get to know our fellow Italians and learn everything we could about their beautiful and artistic culture, so every weekend we'd hit the road. We soaked up all the cultural opportunities we could: modern art, classical opera, architecture, and of course plenty of pasta and pizza. On Saturdays my family and I went to the museums, eventually visiting every one in Rome and Florence and even one or two in Milan as well as the Villa Borghese, a seventeenth-century villa turned museum on the edge of Rome that now houses an amazing art collection. On Sundays we'd tour small villages and the Italian countryside. We kept learning.

That all helped me when I started Hikma. I already had that foundation of knowledge of different cultures and business practices. I knew what to expect in different regions of the world.

For example, we know our Hikma clients in Europe and the Middle East tend to make us wait close to a year for payment, but our US-based clients pay us within two to three months. It's a cultural difference for which we've had to adjust. We also know our private-sector clients pay more quickly than our government clients.

We've also learned that in some countries the boss's word is almost sacred. If he or she makes a mistake, the workers or management won't correct it. They believe if their boss says it, it must be right—even when it's wrong. Some cultural hierarchies are so well established, it's impossible to make any kind of sale without the boss's consent.

But we've also learned that in countries such as China,

hierarchies can be broken at least temporarily. I've seen a driver join his CEO for lunch, and there's mutual respect.

The point is if you're going to sell millions of products in different countries, you really have to understand the people who buy them.

America taught me to think big, and Eli Lilly furthered my learning. That education helped me as well as the company achieve success. In the twelve years I was with Eli Lilly, our sales in the Middle East ballooned from US$150,000 in 1964 to US$15 million in 1976. My formal and on-the-job educations helped me create a winning formula.

I was then able to build upon that knowledge and use it as the foundation for my own corporation.

Learning from Others

When I started Hikma, I had to keep learning at an accelerated rate right along with my new employees. There weren't many of us. In fact there were fewer of us than there were machines in our production process. We had a lot to learn and a short amount of time in which to do it.

From the beginning Hikma had licensing from Japan for injectable medications. But we wanted to introduce our own generic drugs—to have copies of the originals but with better service and the same efficacy at lower prices. To achieve that we located healthy volunteers and conducted our own comparative studies against the originators' products. We were the first company in the MENA region to do that—and we even made sure we adhered to FDA guidelines, which were the strictest anywhere, even though that wasn't necessary for what we were doing. But we wanted to go that extra mile voluntarily and map out our route for the future.

We wanted to keep learning and keep testing for more-advanced results, so we contacted officials at Jordan's Ministry of Health for their approval to open a center exclusively for our comparative studies. That kind of testing had never been done locally before, but the MOH quickly recognized the benefits of our research and gave their approval.

Once we'd officially opened the center, we needed to find subjects. We contacted a professor at the Jordan University of Science and Technology (JUST), where some of our employees had gone to school, and he put out a call for student volunteers. One of the feasibility and efficacy studies we wanted to conduct on them was for the effectiveness of our antibiotics. The students were more than happy to have free health-care treatment, and we were happy to have willing human participants. We learned from them.

Never stop learning.

LESSON THREE

Communicate Well

As I stood in front of the students gathered in the auditorium in West Hall, American University of Beirut's student center, I was feeling a bit jittery. I always did just before speaking publicly. But once I started delivering my speech, the nervousness left me, and I felt confident as only a full-of-himself, twenty-year-old male who thought he knew everything could be.

I'd been practicing my public speaking, refining it during the eighteen months I'd been at AUB, and as toastmaster of one of the student societies, I was feeling pretty proud of myself. Life would soon begin to show me how much I still needed to learn, but at that time I thought I knew it all, as do most young men even today. I think it's an age and gender trait.

At the end of my speech, my inflated opinion of myself was confirmed when I stepped down from the stage and a tall, stunning girl walked up to me.

"You have a nice voice," she said and smiled sweetly.

Instantly my head inflated a bit more. I'd communicated well enough to attract the attention of a dark-eyed beauty with long, wavy hair.

So what was my follow-up to the complement from the amazingly gorgeous coed? Feeling overly bold, I asked, "Is that the only nice thing you see in me?"

She laughed, blushed, and walked away. And I didn't follow her.

Communication failure.

But that girl was now on my radar. I found myself constantly looking for her on campus and finally spotted her a few days later sitting near me in the university's chapel. We had short daily prayer sessions there, and I was enormously pleased that day to look over and discover the new woman of my dreams. She had the most incredibly beautiful face I'd ever seen. She left me speechless.

Communication failure. Again.

Despite the bravado I normally displayed, for some reason I was too afraid to speak to her. What was more, since we had assigned seating, I realized with chagrin, she must have been sitting there for months and I'd never even noticed her, too caught up in my studies and my own interests to pay attention to the natural beauty that was obviously just a few feet away from me.

Observation failure.

Finally one day I worked up my courage, waited for her after chapel, and, tamping down my ego as I took a big gulp of humility, said softly, "Hello. My name is Samih Darwazah."

"I know," she said. "I remember you from the West Hall event. You still have a nice voice."

Communication success.

So what happened to that gorgeous girl? I continued our communication—and married her. How's that for the ultimate success?

Learning to communicate well is critical to your success in life and especially in any entrepreneurial endeavors you'll undertake. It's a skill I've continued to improve upon over the years—more continued learning, as I mentioned in the last chapter. But communication is a subject so important, it warrants its own chapter.

Whether it's dealing one on one with someone, writing, or speaking in front of people in groups as small as five in a boardroom or as large as thousands at a commencement exercise or conference, you need to learn how to communicate accurately to get your point across.

One-on-One Relationships

Long ago I learned the power of personal relationships and how much they need to be based on trust. That knowledge served me well when I started my own company, Hikma. No matter how virtual our business world becomes, I always believe personal relationships and face-to-face meetings are more meaningful than e-mail because you can read others' body language—a form of communication that sometimes is much louder than the words coming from their mouths.

That's why, when I sit in a room with potential clients, investors, or partners, I like to have light illuminating their faces so I can clearly see the details of their expressions. I want to know if they like what I'm talking about—or if they want to throw me out. Are they glancing at their watches because they're bored with what I'm saying? If I see something like that, it's my hint to switch to a more-interesting subject.

Meetings at a potential supplier's or partner's office also give me chances to check out their cleanliness or lack thereof; in the pharmaceutical business, where contamination of any kind can be deadly, that's important to learn. How clean they and their office are tells me a lot about how they operate.

That's why a one-on-one connection can be so important—and revealing.

Networking

I've attended a lot of conferences and social events in my life. The most productive, both personally and professionally, are those where I've tried to make human connections with people and not worried about what they could do for me. Usually I'll go into an event looking for specific people I want to get to know better.

That's networking—an important form of communication.

It's not hand pumping your way through a crowd, spewing a ten-second elevator speech about who you are in order to make sales. Instead networking is building close relationships based on friendship—getting to know people, their families, the details of their jobs and companies, what their concerns are, how they spend their free time. It's being willing to help them and being more concerned with what's going on in their lives than about the bottom line on your profit statement. That's much deeper than just faking a smile to make a sale.

But here's the thing: when you establish those relationships and maintain them through the years, really cultivate them, many times they will reward you financially and professionally. Why? Because the people in your network have learned to trust you and will, in turn, reward you with their business.

And, as the saying goes, it's not what you know but who you know. Once you've made that in-person connection and maintained it, consider taking your networking into cyberspace with online social media. Research shows more and more corporate executives are looking to websites such as LinkedIn when they want to recruit quality candidates for their companies' job openings, expand their reaches, or make sales. They look to their connections, the network of people they know and have worked with, or their connections' associates. That's because if you're like most people, those you know or those your friends can vouch for are more trustworthy than people who are total unknowns.

Communicating with Employees

Some of the most important communication you'll do every day is with your employees and coworkers. It's critical that you master not only how you say something but your tone. And always remember: employees want their bosses to respect them, value them, and hear what they're saying.

Hikma has a policy of evaluating employees at least twice a year. Ideally one of our managers will sit down with a worker and give an honest appraisal of his or her progress since the previous evaluation. The two should be able to discuss openly strengths and weaknesses in order to figure out how the employee's weaker points can be improved.

If the manager doesn't handle these evaluations well, employees may become defensive, which is counterproductive. We train our managers to present fact-based comments as much as possible as positively as possible. I'm very open about offering critiques on potential areas for improvement because I think they're learning opportunities even if employees aren't always happy to receive them.

I've found through experience that it's usually better to avoid questions beginning with the word *why* because it sounds so accusatory and puts the person on the defensive. We prefer to ask employees *how*. We want to know how can we improve this, how can we change that. When questions are posed in a positive and open-ended way like that, they usually have better results. Employees are much more willing to accept them with better attitudes if they don't feel they have to defend themselves. If review and evaluation sessions are handled correctly, many times you'll find employees will make the necessary changes on their own.

I know some companies' executives abuse employee evaluations, especially if an employee's contract specifies raises based on performance. If profits are down, and the company isn't able to give employees raises, sometimes executives will conceal that and will instead fabricate poor performance for the evaluations as an excuse to keep workers at the same pay scale.

I don't believe in doing business that way. There was a time in the 1990s when Hikma couldn't give raises. We were cash poor from the rapid expansions we'd made, but we were honest in our communications with our employees and told them exactly what was going on. They understood and hung in there with us. Once the belt tightening was over, they received their raises.

But you must have a track record of being honest with your workers. If you don't, your valuable employees may not be willing to ride out your financial difficulties and instead may start looking for work elsewhere in order to get the money they feel they deserve. If they know they've done good jobs and believe you're fabricating their poor-performance evaluations just to get out of giving them raises, you run the risk of alienating them, which never has good results.

You also have to be careful about the way you communicate with your employees—not only with the tone of your voice but also in your choice of words. It's important to make sure those you work with understand exactly what you're saying.

You also have to put on your psychologist's hat and realize what different personalities your employees have. They all come from different backgrounds and have varying degrees of sensitivity. Someone may process information you gave him or her at face value, but another may react very differently and take offense. Communication is a tricky thing. Honestly, sometimes it's like walking on eggshells when you're dealing with very sensitive people.

I'd once told a woman on our staff, "We're very good at promoting our products to physicians, but we're not that good at promoting over-the-counter drugs to the public. You should take a social-marketing course to learn how to do that."

The pharmaceutical field had only recently started using social marketing such as advertising in magazines and on television as well as the emerging social media of Twitter and Facebook. I wanted to stay one step ahead of the competition and have someone at Hikma find out more about it and show us how to implement it.

Either I didn't say it right, or the employee was feeling overly sensitive. Whatever the reason, we didn't communicate well with each other, and she missed my point about Hikma's learning more about social media. Instead she thought I was upset with her and her job performance.

The next day she came to talk to me, and she was not happy.

"You said I wasn't good at promoting our over-the-counter drugs," she said, visibly upset.

"No, I said you are excellent, but you could use a little work in a *new* field, that's all," I said.

She calmed down a bit and asked, "Do you really think it's worth the money to send me to London for a one-day course?"

"Yes, because it'll open doors for you and the company," I said.

That must have been the key phrase that clicked with her. When she finally realized I wasn't criticizing her performance, she agreed to take the course and headed off to London for her continuing education.

Communication success.

Electronic Communication

Computers and the Internet are vitally important in today's business world. However, though e-mail certainly can be a time saver and provides an efficient way to communicate quickly, it's also somewhat kicked interpersonal skills and etiquette to the curb. Even with e-mail you have to mind your manners and be nice to people.

Especially with business-related correspondence, you need to answer in a timely manner. I try to acknowledge and respond to any correspondence I receive as quickly as possible. When someone e-mails me an invitation, I make sure to answer if only to thank them for the honor of including me. I may not be able or want to attend the event, but it's just common courtesy to answer a sender and not make him or her feel like you're ignoring him or her. If you don't respond, that sends a message of its own: that you consider this person so unimportant, you can't even take a few seconds to be bothered with sending him or her a reply. Of course there are some people with whom you may deliberately choose not to continue communication for various reasons, but that's another topic.

Today there's no excuse not to respond to business inquiries whether you choose to do it via e-mail, text, or cell phone. It's so much easier than it used to be. You don't have the time delays of "snail mail" or other old-school forms of communication.

At Hikma in the late 1970s, we used an early version of text messaging and faxing called a Telex—a printer that was like a telephone network. You would type someone a message and send it, then soon the same machine would type out the other person's reply. Sounds pretty antiquated, doesn't it? But at the time we were cutting edge with that technology and thrilled with the fast response time.

Learn to Write

If you're planning to advance up the corporate ladder, you'd better learn how to write. That means communicating in well-constructed sentences with proper grammar and punctuation. And if you're already an executive or business owner, you might want to double check what kind of writing image your employees are presenting to your customers. It could be an eye-opening experience. You might be surprised to discover how many clients are rejecting your company because your employees' bad writing makes them—and you by association—appear to be not well educated. Who would want to purchase a product from a company that hires barely literate people?

A common complaint supervisors at many corporations have is they can't understand employees' memos and e-mails because the writing and sentence structure are so poor. Grammarly, a San-Francisco-based company that sells grammar, spelling, proofreading, and plagiarism software, did a study to determine if poor writing had affected the number of promotions people had received in a ten-year period. Grammarly selected one hundred professionals in the consumer packaged-goods industry whose online profiles were posted on LinkedIn and analyzed how many grammar mistakes were in their profiles. Brad Hoover, the CEO of Grammarly, said there were virtually no spelling mistakes in the online profiles probably because of automatic spell check in most writing software and on the LinkedIn website, but grammar errors and misuses of common words were glaring in some of the profiles.

Next Grammarly took a look at the number of times those one hundred people had been promoted and to what levels. The company's analysis revealed those who'd been promoted six to nine times and achieved higher positions had fewer grammatical errors in their profiles than the ones who'd received only one to four promotions during the same period.

That's right: your bad grammar may have cost you a promotion. Between the poor-quality education many students around the world are receiving today and their inability to write basic sentences, good writing is taking a beating, especially punctuation. Today, run-on sentences lacking commas, periods, and question marks are common. Combine that with people's frequent use of street slang, poor spelling, and bad habits from abbreviating for texting on their phones or fitting comments into 140-character tweets, and you realize why some of your employees may not be putting your company's best foot forward with existing or potential clients.

A few years ago the US-based College Board and its National Commission on Writing panel surveyed 120 prominent American companies. The results showed at least one-third of corporate employees, including managers, wrote poorly. If it's that bad in the United States, which has a 99 percent literacy rate (according to the US Central Intelligence Agency's World Factbook), imagine how bad it is in corporations throughout the rest of the world.

Do yourself and your corporation a favor: take a few writing or grammar courses, and do some self-study if you're lacking that skill. As a backup take the time and pay the extra money if necessary to hire an extremely literate executive assistant who can proofread and correct all your correspondence. That's your public face to the world. Make sure you're communicating your company's message as grammatically perfectly as possible.

The Importance of Public Speaking

I definitely recommend you take a public-speaking class at some time in your life, whether in college or as part of continuing your adult education.

Speaking in front of groups forces you to organize and itemize your ideas clearly and find the best, most efficient way to make others understand them and your point of view—before you lose your audience's interest. You learn to think on your feet, to gauge the effects your message is having on listeners (or whether they're no longer listening), and to change certain aspects of your speech if you feel you're not helping people understand the points you're making. Most important, public speaking teaches you to find your own voice.

That's a skill you have to master if you want to rise through the ranks as an executive. If you have any fear of it, you'd better find a way to get over it, and the best way I know to do that is to stand up in front of a large group, even if your knees are knocking, and just start talking. You must be able to communicate your ideas to large groups of people.

Write down your talking points, and make sure they're important—don't just babble on endlessly about irrelevant things. State a problem, and give your solutions. Have a beginning, a middle, and an end. Be passionate and sincere, throw in a good opening joke, then rehearse, rehearse, rehearse.

When it comes time to deliver your speech, don't be boring and drone on or read your notes in a monotone. *Please* don't read your notes in a monotone. Your audience doesn't want you to put them to sleep. Get your nose out of your notes, and look up at everyone then scan the audience to take in different parts of the room as you connect eye to eye with various people.

Stand up straight, and stop rocking back and forth. You don't want to make your audience seasick. Be animated and enthusiastic, but don't deliver your speech like an out-of-control jackhammer. Instead slow down and remember to breathe. You don't want to get lightheaded from a lack of oxygen and pass out onstage. That could be embarrassing.

Emphasize your keywords, and pause after you make an important point, but when you do so don't fill that empty space with "ummm." I recommend taping yourself so you can check to see whether you're ummm-ing to fill the voids.

Be real and human. Most of all remember to smile and occasionally laugh and joke. Nobody likes a sour-looking speaker.

Communicating with a large audience isn't easy, but it is necessary for your career growth. Besides my public speaking at AUB, I gained more experience when Samira and I were talking about Jordan to groups in the United States during my Fulbright year. Though at times Samira and I would speak without the other being there, I found when we were addressing an audience as a couple, we offered a more complete picture. She would mention something I hadn't thought of or I'd forgotten and vice versa. We spontaneously linked off each other's remarks, and just having her next to me gave me a great deal of confidence. It made me more relaxed, and it allowed us to joke around with each other and the people before us, prompting the audience to interact with us and enjoy the discussion more. If you can begin your public-speaking career with someone close to you as your partner, it will make your experience so much easier.

Besides being fun and allowing us to meet some wonderful people, speaking to those groups of Americans also gave me confidence that prepared me for my job interviews with prospective employers. When Eli Lilly hired me, I started honing my speaking skills even more as I learned to make presentations. Since then I've been asked to address numerous entrepreneurial and pharmaceutical-related conferences around the world. I've become a seasoned public speaker whether I wanted to or not. I've had to.

Speaking in front of crowds is never easy, not even now in my eighty-third year. Every time I get up onstage and look down at all the faces, I experience a brief moment of panic before I start speaking—just as I did when I was that twenty-year-old student at AUB. But now I find once I get into the core of whatever message I'm delivering, I lose that fear and become caught up in the ideas I want to communicate.

I have to admit, some speeches I've given have received better reviews than others. In the late 1980s, I was attending a conference in Amman with about a hundred representatives from other manufacturing companies. At that time there was a push in the industry to ask for Jordanian governmental support and protection, especially with economic treaties for companies that were exporting to other nations.

As one of the featured speakers, I told the group I didn't agree, that we shouldn't ask for that kind of protection because we didn't need it. Our companies and the quality products we manufactured should be able to stand alone on the world stage. We should work hard to become so good, we didn't need a government to protect us as if we were infants who had to be coddled and were fighting to survive against the "unfair" onslaught of big, bad corporations.

I said that instead, we should allow the push of competition to encourage lower-quality companies to improve themselves in order to match the quality of the stronger corporations. We needed self-improvement, not hand holding.

I wasn't saying what the majority wanted to hear, and I knew it. As I looked down at the audience from the stage, I could see in their faces a somewhat hostile attitude. I could have said what they wanted to hear. Instead I was communicating what ethically I felt they *needed* to hear. At that moment I ignored the angry faces and tried to explain to them why they needed to reconsider their viewpoints. I wasn't giving that speech because I wanted to be liked or to become the most popular person at the conference. I was giving it because that was what manufacturers in Jordan really needed. We all needed to become better, quality-oriented companies, not slackers just barely getting by or even manufacturing products that might affect our consumers' health in adverse ways.

My speech was met with stony, icy silence. I mean you could have heard crickets chirping it was so quiet. About five people supported me out of the hundred in attendance.

It appeared I'd had another communication failure, at least in terms of my peers who had their own agendas. But the speech wasn't a total failure. I continued to repeat it for the next few years, and a few people were listening. Officials working for the Jordanian government heard me and agreed with me, so in that aspect I succeeded.

I've also had the opportunity to deliver some joyful speeches where the audiences were definitely supportive. When my alma mater, St. Louis College of Pharmacy, bestowed an honorary doctorate on me in May 2010, forty-six years after I'd received my master's there, and asked me to deliver the commencement address to hundreds of graduates and their families, I was filled with emotion as I looked down at my family's smiling faces. I'd followed my dream to St. Louis, and my entire family had supported me—from my wife and children to my brothers who'd helped take care of my pharmacy in Amman.

Bottom line, I couldn't have done it without their support, especially my wife's and children's. They had agreed to pack up and move halfway around the world to a strange, new country. Thankfully, following my dream has benefited all of us. My family forms the foundation of any success I've been able to build upon in life.

I told the graduating class their dreams could prove to be their driving forces, but dreams are always bigger than what a single person can accomplish alone. I told them to follow their dreams but have plans in place to achieve their goals then attack those goals with action. Dreams mean nothing if you're not prepared to take action to put them into effect.

My speech must not have been too horrible: the college invited me back to speak to the graduates the following year too, which was indeed a true honor.

Learn the Value of Marketing, Market Research, and Feasibility Studies

Besides learning how to communicate to crowds with public speaking, you need to learn to communicate with individuals on a mass scale. The two may seem like the same thing, but they're vastly different. That's because the latter is marketing—making sure your products speak to and connect with individuals so successfully, those customers will return again and again to buy from you. And obviously the more customers you can convince to buy from you globally, as long as your price point also speaks to them and your overhead is abundantly covered, the more profitable your corporation will be.

When I started working at Eli Lilly, my education followed a sharp growth curve, especially in the area of marketing products. I'd first learned of the concept at St. Louis College of Pharmacy, but I didn't really begin to understand the difference between selling a product and selling it smartly until I got to Eli Lilly.

I was fortunate to have attended a university in the United States then landed a job with an American-based company. I say fortunate because nobody does marketing quite as well as American businesses, probably because the concept of marketing research started at US universities as early as 1895. That was when researchers at the University of Minnesota mailed questionnaires to people asking for their opinions on advertising. Ten years later the University of Pennsylvania offered a course in marketing products.

But the field really started making viable inroads in 1932, when George Gallup became the director of research at the New York advertising agency Young & Rubicam. Within three years he'd started his own company to focus on advertising research and political polling—the beginning of the United States well-known Gallup Polls.

By the time I'd graduated from St. Louis College in 1964, companies were beginning to realize they needed to understand not only who their potential customers were but what they wanted. That affected pricing, packaging, branding, and how to beat the competition.

Marketing isn't something I could have learned in the Middle East. People there know how to haggle, trade, and negotiate well. Nobody's better or tougher from the bazaars to the boardroom since many come from families of merchants and traders. Selling is in their blood. However, they don't really recognize the broader need for marketing and marketing research. Without them it's difficult to take a business to a global level, and Eli Lilly definitely furthered my education in that area.

Rather than just throwing your products out into the marketplace and fervently hoping people will buy them, marketing is getting inside your customers' heads in advance. It's understanding your customers so well before your products are released on the open market that you know where, when, and at what price they will buy your items—or any item.

It's taking the theory of academic knowledge, such as research and feasibility studies, and, as accurately as possible, translating that into reality—the fluid, ever-changing world of buying, selling, and customer fickleness. One minute customers want this, but three months later they want something else. You have to stay one step ahead of their changing viewpoints, which the various media—especially movies, television, and commercials—are constantly manipulating and influencing.

The communication called marketing means your company discovers the needs and wants of your potential customers, accurately forecasts their future buying trends, then makes sure your products satisfy and surpass those needs. It's a calculated risk, but doing no marketing is just plain risky.

You have to communicate the right questions to the right people then evaluate the answers to get the right result. Without that you run the risk of losing a lot of your company's money.

By the time I left Eli Lilly in 1976 to start Hikma, I was a total fan of market research. The first thing I did was take six months to complete a study to determine if a new pharmaceutical company based in Jordan and serving the Middle East was even feasible in terms of profitability and demand. I asked a lot of key people a lot of questions. Communication was critical. I had to learn if there were a market for the products I hoped to sell. Fortunately there was (and still is).

But that wasn't the end. I still had to decide what products Hikma would manufacture. Again I asked a lot of questions and did a six-month study to find out what the market needs were and what customers wanted in terms of pricing and quality. What I discovered was the region had a large need for antibiotics.

I decided not to go with penicillin even though it was popular at the time. Instead I started with the manufacture of cephalosporins, or drugs that were used to fight a wide variety of bacterial infections especially after surgery. That was because my market research had included pharmaceutical journals that indicated this was the direction many companies were beginning to go. It seemed to be the future of the industry at least for the next five to ten years, and thankfully that proved to be correct. Many new cephalosporins have emerged in the past thirty years while very few new penicillins have appeared since the 1980s. Communicating the right questions to the right people and doing the necessary market research helped me learn enough to select the best product.

Hikma has changed slightly in the way we do market research today. We still conduct our own studies; we're still asking questions and listening carefully to the answers. But now we also purchase industry reports to get information for upcoming product lines. Since day one I've always believed we should base our decisions on the best information available, taking calculated risks instead of flying blindly through the marketplace.

Sales

Eli Lilly taught me you don't need a lot of hype and sales skills to sell a product in which you truly believe. That lesson carried over when I founded Hikma. If I didn't believe in the products we sold, my company never would have survived.

Having a technique and sharpening your sales skills are fine, but don't replace passion for what you're selling and belief in the quality of your products. Hikma's management team and salespeople have to preach what they believe. In one sense I've made that easy for them. We have extremely high in-house quality control because the Hikma name means more than short-term profits. From the time I founded the company, I've made it clear to all our employees we don't just talk quality, we live it.

Years ago, when the quality-control person at one of our manufacturing plants tested a batch of pharmaceuticals, the results indicated the drugs didn't meet our established standards. The employee performed the tests again on the same batch just to make sure it wasn't a mistake, but the results were the same. When she came to me to tell me, I ordered the entire batch of medication be destroyed even though it was worth more than US$50,000.

That sounds like a lot of money, and it was, but you have to realize your name and that of your company are worth more. Your reputation shouts when it communicates, but only you can determine what that communication is going to be. Do your employees and customers expect your products always to be high quality? Do they know your business dealings are always honest and honorable? If so that's worth far more than a batch of destroyed products. Your good name is priceless.

Or are you skimming by with the least-acceptable-quality products? If so, I guarantee you, that's communicating a lot too.

I'd much rather maintain Hikma's reputation and integrity than settle for short-term profits. And I never, ever want any of our products to endanger our customers. Quality is the most important thing when it comes to our pharmaceuticals. Here's the Hikma rule: if we feel comfortable giving a medication to our sons and daughters, we'll release it for our customers to use. If we wouldn't give it to our families because we aren't comfortable with the quality, we don't release the product.

When it comes to what you sell, it's all about quality, not compromise.

Make sure your communication on all levels shows the public just how quality minded your company is.

LESSON FOUR

Marry Wisely

When I first met the woman who would become my wife, she didn't fit into my life plan. At the time I was enthusiastically concentrating on my studies at American University in Beirut, thankful I could even go to college after my family and I had become refugees. I was also enjoying frequent political and philosophical dialogues with my professors and fellow students.

I knew I wanted to get married and start a family at some point, but at twenty years old I wasn't looking for a wife—or even a steady girlfriend. Being one of the two stars in a wedding production was definitely the last thing on my mind. I wanted to start my career, make some money, travel a bit to feed my growing wanderlust, and eventually start saving for the day I'd get married.

Then this dark-eyed beauty walked up to me and told me I had a nice voice. Bam! I threw that life schedule right out the window.

Samira Fadli was a Palestinian refugee too. She and her family had been living in Jerusalem, but after her father was killed in partisan fighting they'd been driven out of their home. The Fadlis had settled in Beirut with Samira's uncle, Abdul Rahman, who'd become the family's guardian. He was an AUB alum and had founded a tea-import company, an entrepreneurial venture that had made him very successful and well known all over Lebanon.

I quickly realized from the time I spent talking to Samira on campus that she was a beauty both inside and out. Her charming smile lit up her dark eyes and reflected a warmth to everyone with whom she came into contact. I was pleased to notice she was also extremely intelligent—a political-science and history major who planned to become a teacher.

The bad news was she was scheduled to graduate within a few months and would soon be leaving AUB. That meant I had to make my move in a hurry and not let her get away.

Because her family, especially her uncle Abdul, was strict and conservative, we could see each other only on campus. There was no dating and definitely no touching. I couldn't even hold her hand.

I'm sure that sounds very old-fashioned to most people. But the fact that Samira and I couldn't have a physical relationship with each other freed us to talk—a lot—about everything. We were able to explore each other's personalities, thoughts, hopes, and dreams to find out if we really were compatible. I feel sorry for those today who rush past that critical part of a relationship and go straight to the physical, only to discover too late they have nothing in common and don't even like each other.

But with Samira I found someone who quickly became my best friend. I couldn't wait to talk to her and share my day with her.

I knew pretty much from the first few days with Samira that she was the one I wanted to be with for the rest of my life. The main reason I didn't propose right away was I had nothing to offer her but hope for the future. I was a poor student who wouldn't graduate for at least another two years (it actually turned out to be three). The best I could do was hold down a part-time job. What was I going to say? "Please marry me and support me until I graduate"? My pride wasn't dealing with that scenario too well.

But the clock was ticking, and I knew once Samira graduated and moved out into the world for a job, there was a strong chance some other man would snatch her away from me. She was practically perfect, so I knew that was a very real possibility. As it was there were many young men on campus vying for her attention. The more I thought about it, the more I couldn't believe my good fortune that she'd chosen to speak to me that day in West Hall. I'm forever thankful she ignored my youthful bravado and recognized who I really was underneath it all.

A few months after we'd met, as Samira was preparing for her graduation, I asked her to marry me. But her answer wasn't what I wanted to hear. She didn't say no, but she didn't say yes either. All she said was I had to ask her uncle's permission—the wealthy and famous Uncle Abdul.

My heart sank. It was bad enough having to swallow my pride to ask Samira to become engaged to me then wait years to get married, until I could graduate and find a job. Trying to sell that to a powerful businessman like Abdul Rahman seemed nearly impossible.

On top of that, Samira's mother was opposed to our marriage. She didn't want her beautiful and talented daughter to waste her life on a penniless student like me.

Finally, at Samira's urging, I went to her uncle Abdul to ask for her hand in marriage. As I stood before him, nervous and shaking, he sized me up but wouldn't give me a yes or no answer. Instead he said the marriage request had to come from my family.

I was crushed but refused to accept defeat. I knew my father, salesman that he was, would make a wonderful impression on Samira's uncle and the rest of her family. He could be very convincing.

Unfortunately my family was as opposed to our marriage as Samira's. It seemed everyone was against us. My father was furious I was even considering marriage before I'd graduated and obtained a job. No matter what I said, I couldn't make him see how special Samira was and that I was desperately afraid I'd lose her if I didn't propose soon. I told him this opportunity for happiness may never come my way again, but he wouldn't change his mind.

I turned to the only person who could sway my father: my mother. I begged her to talk to him and convince him not only to give his approval but to travel to Beirut to meet with Samira's family.

I'm not sure what my mother said, but my father finally did give his approval of my marriage. Just as I was beginning to think things might work out, my dreams were dashed again when I learned he refused to go to Lebanon to speak with Samira's family. Again my mother used her charms on him, and this time he agreed at least to allow *her* to travel to Beirut with my older brother, Khaled. It wasn't what I'd hoped for, but it was something.

Uncle Abdul must have liked what my mother and brother said to him because he finally gave his approval, and by the end of the summer Samira and I were officially engaged. That meant we could date, but we had to have a chaperone every time we went somewhere together.

Our small wedding took place a year later, in October 1952, just as I was turning twenty-two. As I write this, my beautiful Samira and I have celebrated almost sixty-one years of marriage. She took a chance on me and always believed I'd achieve great things. It's because of her faith in me and her constant encouragement that I've achieved any success not only in my career but in life.

Make sure you marry well. If you do, there's no telling how high you'll soar.

Choose Someone Who's Willing to Work Hard and Isn't All about the Money

The qualities and personality traits that might bond two people to each other may not work for two others, but there are some things to consider if you're planning to become a global entrepreneur.

You stand a better chance of having a happy marriage if you can find someone who will be loyal to you and emotionally supportive even if you're not wealthy.

If you are an entrepreneur and are planning to expand your business overseas, you're probably going to have some very lean years until you start making a profit. As a matter of fact, in the first few years you'll probably be paying your employees and not taking a paycheck yourself—just as I did. That's one good reason to have a spouse who will hang in there with you when you're trying not to panic about how to pay the constant stream of bills.

Samira and I had a few dirt-poor years when we were first married and later when I started Hikma. Right after our marriage,

Samira started working as an English and Arabic teacher at a children's school, so what I had dreaded most did happen: my wife had to support me for a few years. Times were tight, but Samira didn't seem to mind. Since both our families had been refugees, we'd experienced financial hardships before, so to some degree we knew we'd survive, and these were only temporary conditions.

Our first home in Beirut was what had been the small servants' quarters of a former mansion that had been converted into apartments. We lived on the fifth floor, and there were no elevators, so we got our exercise trudging up and down the stairs every day. Our nightly meals were almost always pasta with various sauces because that was the cheapest food we could buy.

I was in school full time but eventually was able to find a part-time teaching job. We were barely paying the bills. Then Samira found out she was pregnant, which was a bit of a shock to us. We both wanted children someday, but they weren't scheduled for another few years.

We knew eventually Samira would have to quit her job, and as she was the one providing most of our financial support, we knew we had to earn extra money to cover the time she'd be home with the baby. Fortunately I found a second part-time teaching job. Between Samira's full-time job and her pregnancy, which drained her energy, and my school workload plus two part-time jobs, we were both exhausted.

Our beautiful little daughter, May, was born in the summer of 1953. Samira was no longer working, so our only money was from what we'd managed to save and my part-time jobs. We thought our financial problems would disappear when I graduated the following spring, but I couldn't find work. There were simply no pharmacy jobs in Beirut.

We moved to Amman to be with my family, but there were no pharmacy jobs there either. Finally, in desperation, Samira and I accepted two teaching positions in Marjyoun, a village in Southern Lebanon. Since we needed childcare for May, we had to leave her in Beirut with Samira's mother during the week. We could spend time with our baby only on weekends, which was heartbreaking.

Through it all Samira remained my most steadfast supporter and partner.

When I did start working as a pharmacist in Kuwait, our income greatly improved, but it dipped again when I quit to buy a pharmacy in Amman. It took a few years to make a profit. Eventually our income improved, and after Eli Lilly hired me we were living very well, especially when we were in Rome. But when I walked away from those nice paychecks in 1976 to start Hikma, we were once again forced to cut back our living expenses and have a very lean lifestyle.

Before I left Eli Lilly, I sat down with my family to discuss the financial sacrifices we'd all have to make. At first Samira wasn't thrilled about having to leave Rome and the stability we had there, especially since we'd just fled the war in Beirut and were still a bit shaken from that. We were just calming down, and now I wanted to throw our lives back into chaos. She was also worried about how we were going to pay for our children's university expenses.

Fortunately May had recently graduated from Purdue University in the United States and was working at her first job. But we still had to pay Said's, Mazen's, and Hana's tuitions. Said was still at Purdue, Mazen was at Lebanese American University in Beirut, and Hana was at International College, a preschool through secondary-level boarding school also located in Beirut that serves as the preparatory school for AUB.

I assured Samira I'd kept money aside to cover our children's tuition and living expenses. I also reminded her that whenever I did leave Lilly, I'd get a hefty financial exit package. I promised her I'd put that aside too for the children's expenses. We had our savings, plus I'd recently sold my pharmacy in Amman and had the proceeds from that.

Once she heard Said's, Mazen's, and Hana's education expenses were covered, I had her complete support.

Still it wasn't easy. Our lifestyle in Amman was very different from the wealth we'd been accustomed to in Rome. Samira and I couldn't even afford to pay rent, so my brothers let me borrow a small apartment they owned. We barely had money to spend on necessities, and there certainly wasn't enough for luxuries such as traveling around the world as we'd done when I worked for Eli Lilly. It was like being students all over again, only this time I had a lot more responsibility, a little less hair, and a bigger family to consider.

It took two years to plan my company and finish building my first pharmaceutical-manufacturing plant in Amman. That's a long time to have a lot of money going out the door, to pay for construction and salaries, and none coming in. Samira had to sacrifice a lot, but she continued to support me and never doubted my decision to own a business.

Take a look at the person you're considering marrying. Would he or she still love you if your money were gone and you had to downsize your living accommodations? What if you couldn't eat as well? What if you lost your house to foreclosure? In today's economy, with many corporations laying off employees, would you and your spouse remain close if you lost your job and couldn't find another one for a few years? What if you both lost your jobs? Would your love last? Would you still be loyal to each other, still encourage your mate even if times were depressing and bad?

Is the person you want to marry high maintenance—someone who was raised in a wealthy family and expects always to have the same lifestyle his or her parents provided while he or she was growing up? Does your partner always expect to live a jet-setting life? Does he or she insist on expensive new clothes and homes in wealthy neighborhoods? Will he or she walk out the door if you're suddenly forced into a more humble lifestyle?

On the other hand, what if you suddenly became very wealthy? Would that change in status affect your spouse in an adverse way? Would he or she become arrogant? Is he or she reasonable about spending money and always living within his or her means? Or would he or she go crazy buying new cars, yachts, and mansions?

These are all questions you need to ask yourself when you're considering marriage. It's best to find someone who will stick by you whether you're wealthy or struggling financially.

Fortunately that's exactly the kind of wife I was able to find. She wanted me to use my abilities in the best way possible, but how much money I made was never a consideration for her. It was always about my happiness and achievement, and I felt the same way about her. Samira and our four children were the reasons I wanted to work hard and build a good life and a successful global enterprise. I didn't want my children to have to endure poverty, homelessness, and uncertainty as my wife and I had when we were refugees. I wanted to make their lives better, to provide futures for them and eventually for my grandchildren as well.

Is that the attitude of the person you want to marry? Do you want to make his or her life better, and does he or she want to improve yours no matter what sacrifices he or she will have to make?

Getting married gave me the determination to reach my goals. I can say without a doubt, Samira is the reason for my success. I could not have done it without her.

Find Someone Who's Growing Your Way

It's important for your mate to be on the same page you are, especially when it comes to career achievement. You have to be *growing* as well as *going* the same way. There has to be unity, working together as a solid team, if you're both going to achieve success.

If you're interested only in the flash of a trophy spouse who looks good, someone to parade around while hoping for the envy of all you meet, you're probably not going to have a very successful marriage—or career path. If your mate can't withstand the heat of reality that comes from being in a relationship with an international businessperson, you and your marriage are going to suffer. My advice is to look for whatever you consider your particular brand of beauty, but definitely combine that with brains. Don't settle for anything less than an intelligent mate.

You've got to have brains to move up through the ranks of an international corporation. If you marry someone who looks good but can't mentally keep up with you, you're going to get bored quickly and start looking elsewhere for someone to share what's going on in your career.

Fortunately I married someone with both brains and beauty. Samira and I are so in sync and of one mind, we not only finish each other's sentences but frequently know in advance what the other one is about to say.

"Remember that road in Beirut?" I said to her one day.

"Oh yes. By that shop."

"Yes. Tell me, was it the man who got married and moved into that building?" I asked.

"No, his brother," she said.

We looked around and saw shaking heads and puzzled looks. Nobody else knew what we were talking about, but our half-sentences and vague references were crystal clear to us.

It's still amazing to me at times when I realize I found someone who is that much in sync with me.

Hopefully, before you married you discovered your mate's dreams for the future and found them compatible with yours. If not you're going to have difficulties. That's why it's so important to do a *lot* of talking before you get married. Ask the critical questions. Find out if what you want is what he or she wants too.

It's important for a married couple to grow together. If you have your eyes set on reaching the top of a mountain but your intended wants only to stay at the base camp and do as little as possible to get by, you're going to clash and have problems throughout your marriage.

Look for someone who wants to grow as much and as quickly as you do. Setting the pace together, like good running partners, is important. You don't want someone who's too far behind you or too far ahead. Instead look for someone who will move out ahead just a little to encourage you to pick up the pace when you're getting tired or discouraged but keep up with you when you get a burst of energy and surge forward.

A critical consideration is whether your mate wants to grow in the same direction you do. You won't achieve much if you're constantly pulling in opposite directions like a tug-of-war. If your spouse is headed east and you're going west, there isn't going to be much harmony. Is he or she willing to jump over onto your path and move forward as a team with you? If you're motivated to advance your career as much as possible, is your mate of the same mindset? If you need to live in London to advance your career, but your mate doesn't want to move out of your safe, familiar neighborhood in Amman, is that going to work? What if he or she needs to move for a job and you don't want that?

My career involved moving all over the world, and Samira always willingly and enthusiastically supported me in that— even if it meant she was going to have to deal with a strange new country, a new language, and new customs and cultures. We both viewed it the same way: as another exciting opportunity to learn more.

What if you need to move, but your spouse refuses? That means you lose a career opportunity (and sometimes that may be the best thing for the entire family), but it could also lead to feelings of resentment, which unfortunately could cause a lot of tension and fighting in your marriage.

Successful entrepreneurs, whether they're men or women, have mates who are incredibly supportive of their goals and ambitions. They're on the same page and provide the emotional support that is so critically important for their spouses to achieve great things.

If you can meet someone early in life and grow together as I did, it will make you stronger and more motivated.

Choose Someone with Good Character

No matter what your career, when you're considering marriage, always look for someone with good character. If the so-called love of your life is prone to lying, gambling, cheating, and substance abuse or is a bit of a kleptomaniac, run away as quickly as possible. Trust me, those aren't temporary things. I guarantee they'll come back to haunt you and make your life miserable.

Take a look at the person you think you're in love with and can't live without. Is he or she frequently getting drunk or even doing illegal drugs? Is he or she out of control at parties or social events? Most college freshmen, away from home for the first time, like to blow off steam and attend a lot of parties. That's fine, but by the time you hit twenty you should be settling down and getting serious about your career and life. Before you graduate from college, and certainly once you're out in the business world, you need to put aside the wasted weekends and grow up.

The person who's still partying a little too hard well into his or her twenties and thirties may have a serious problem—one you'll have to deal with if he or she continues that lifestyle and you marry him or her. Don't think you can fix someone like this. Marry only someone you can live with as he or she is, no changes necessary.

You don't want someone who gambles away his or her entire paycheck. You don't want someone who drinks heavily, gets in a car, and runs the risk of killing someone. Avoid like the plague marrying someone who escapes reality with hallucinogenic drugs, because he or she stands a good chance of not advancing his or her career and even ending up in jail.

The good character and good name that come from living a proper life are priceless. Those are qualities you should look for in a mate.

Find an Independent Person You Want to Be with All the Time

It's important to choose a mate who's strong enough to function competently all alone when you're not there. You need to know he or she can handle every emergency as well as the day-to-day issues. But by the same token, you should want to be with that person all the time, and he or she should want to be with you.

Working for a global corporation like Eli Lilly then starting Hikma meant I spent many years in airports and hotels. I traveled a lot, and because we had four children, most of the time Samira couldn't go with me. But I never really worried about her or our family.

That's because I knew she was capable of running our household alone when I wasn't there even though we both preferred doing it as a team. What would I have done if she'd fallen apart every time I left town? Knowing I could count on her to handle everything alone freed me up to do what business I needed to without worrying about my family. It was extremely comforting.

When I was traveling for Eli Lilly, our four children were young, and Samira had to stay home with them. She had to be the disciplinarian, had to sit with them until they completed their homework correctly, and had to enforce the "no television" rule on weekdays because that was the time she'd designated for schoolwork and family.

Even when we were apart for a while, Samira and I always knew we could trust each other. That makes for a very secure marriage, but it does take some effort. It means you need to stay in contact even if you're half a world away. Even when I was in the same city but working long hours, I made sure to spend time with Samira. I wanted to. I *needed* to. She's the one who's always kept me steady and on course.

When our first Hikma factory was under construction, Samira would stop by to make sure conditions were clean and healthy. She also looked after our employees, at times showing up even before I did. We always ate lunch together at the building site.

But when we started doing test runs to manufacture an antibiotic, Samira developed an allergy to some of the ingredients. That barred her from coming inside the plant anymore, but it didn't put an end to our lunches. Instead I went home every day to eat with her. We still make it a point to have lunch together every day except when I'm abroad on business.

Even then I stay in touch and always make sure I'm home on

weekends. I phone Samira every day to see if she's doing OK. We have our little routine we've been saying to each other for years— our secret code.

"Are you happy?" I ask her when I call.

"Of course I am, Samih," she says.

"You are? Then you don't want me to come home?" I tease.

"Yes, yes, I do! Come now!" she says.

I never get tired of hearing her say that no matter how many trips I take. Hana says she can tell when it's me on the phone from the way Samira blushes when we talk.

On Valentine's Day 2013, I was in New York City on business, but I made sure sixty roses were delivered to Samira—one for each year we'd been married. She's had my heart practically from the moment we first met.

Our children and grandchildren tell us they're in awe of our relationship. It's taken work over the years. Nothing comes easily. We've had a happy marriage because both Samira and I have always made it a point to schedule time for each other. We want to spend time together, and we want each other's input on everything.

Mazen's son, Walid, said he still sees the spark between Samira and me. He notices the small things, like when he was driving in Portugal with us a few years back, and I kept resting my hand on her leg. Samira and I still have good chemistry, probably because we've always fueled each other's dreams and ambitions.

May's daughter, Zeena, says she uses our relationship as a guide for finding a husband but gets discouraged because she can't find a man who lives up to her expectations and treats her the same way I treat Samira. Or that could be her excuse to enjoy her single life a bit longer.

No matter what, I don't want my grandchildren to settle for anyone. They need to find the right mates for them—partners who will encourage them as much as Samira and I encourage each other.

Find Someone Who's Outgoing and Forgiving and Has a Good Sense of Humor

Owning a global corporation or even working for one means you and your spouse are going to meet a lot of new people. Make sure whoever you marry is outgoing and likes people. If you're attracted to a shy wallflower, I don't think he or she is going to enjoy traveling the world and meeting all your business associates. Does he or she sit there like a lump at dinner without talking to any of the other guests? Your spouse's interactions with your potential clients, your bosses, and your coworkers can make or break a deal for you.

Make sure you observe your loved one in a lot of social situations before you make the commitment of marriage. See how he or she interacts with your friends and with the strangers who are connected to your job. Is he or she interested in other people? Does he or she ask them questions about their lives, or is he or she too self-absorbed and want to talk only about himself or herself? Can he or she subtlety draw out any critical information you may need without causing a major conflict for you? Can he or she keep up sparkling, fun conversations equally as well as serious, intelligent ones? Is he or she well versed in current events and in your industry? Are people sorry to say good-bye to him or her, or are they happy to see your mate leave?

Another thing to consider is how understanding and forgiving your potential mate is. Does he or she focus on what matters most, or does he or she nitpick every small detail? Everyone makes mistakes, but just like in business, it takes trust, transparency, and respect to make a relationship strong.

That means also having a good sense of humor. Keeping things light and joking about minor things can lead to a smoother relationship. Don't worry about the small things.

One year when our entire family was going on vacation together, Samira and I picked up May's daughters, Zeena and Deema, at the airport. On the drive back to where we were all staying, I sailed right past our exit.

Samira gave me a puzzled look, wondering where I was going.

"Samih, you were supposed to get off there," she said, wondering if I had a surprise trip planned for the four of us or if I were just not paying attention.

I turned to her and said, "Tell me, Samira, how can I focus on the road when such beauty is sitting beside me?"

Ha! Good answer, right? Better not to get offended when someone calls out your shortcomings. Humor can definitely keep fights to a minimum.

If you can, find someone with a sense of humor.

Find Your Perfect Match

When Zeena was a teenager, Samira told her, "You'll know when you meet your true partner in life."

She was right. Practically from the first moment I had seen her, I'd known I'd found mine. That partnership has continued for more than sixty years, resulting in four innovative products (our children), eleven subsidiaries (grandchildren), and a global corporation in seventeen countries. My marriage has been my most successful merger by far.

From the time I started my own company, I've always had a partner—Samira. Hikma wouldn't have been successful without her. It wouldn't have even been built because I would have had no real motivation or support to do it. My family is what fuels my success. The company is for them and their children as well as my employees and their children.

Hire Wisely

After many feasibility studies and much planning, I bought land in Amman, where I wanted to build my first pharmaceutical plant. The building process for me was almost unbearably long and slow. Rationally I knew building a startup from scratch would not be a quick process, but I was impatient, and it seemed as if time were standing still most days. I wanted to be in production, manufacturing medications, but there were so many steps that needed to be completed before we could flip the switch, turn on the machines, and start rolling.

I hired temporary workers to build the factory but, ever mindful of the costs, kept the crew to a minimum. We needed only five cars for the twenty of us to carpool to the job site. We'd start working around six in the morning and keep going until it was dark, which meant some days were fourteen hours long. I loved every enthusiastic worker, every engineer, but each evening after I'd thanked them for the day's work, I'd silently bang my head against a wall, wondering what I could do to make them hurry up and finish.

I needed more help, so I turned to one person I knew would be an asset at the site. It was the spring of 1978, and my older son, Said, was finishing up another year of his studies at Purdue University in the United States. I asked him if he would come to Amman for a month during his summer vacation and help us. Not only did I want to spend time with my son, but I also wanted him to start getting involved in a company I hoped to turn over to him one day.

One of the first jobs I gave Said was building the roof and

installing the skylights. I wasn't worried about his safety. First of all he was very agile and athletic, very sure footed. Not only that but from the time he'd been young, he'd always been very careful and deliberate about everything he did; he was a very thoughtful, highly intelligent person. He'd started talking when he was only about six or seven months old—far earlier than most toddlers. I knew he'd be careful not only with his safety but with the intricate construction required at the plant. He never rushed to cut corners in order to finish a job quickly.

I was so proud knowing my son's hands were helping to build my factory.

Unfortunately, when Samira stopped by she happened to look up and almost had a heart attack when she saw Said on the roof. Convinced he would fall off and be killed, she turned the full force of her anger and fear on me as only a worried mother could do.

"He's starting at the top," I joked, trying to calm her down. "I thought you'd be pleased."

Her icy glare clearly demonstrated she was not amused.

I reminded her how careful and in control Said always was with everything. Eventually she calmed down. As I'd predicted Said successfully finished installing the skylights without taking a swan dive off the roof.

Finally in December 1978, almost two years after I'd resigned from Eli Lilly, our very first Hikma plant was fully operational. We were up and running, only the third manufacturing plant in all of Jordan. I was forty-eight years old, and my second entrepreneurial venture was just beginning. Let that be a lesson: you're never too old to start your own company.

Now came the most important step: staffing my company. I couldn't afford to hire a person to head up Hikma's human-resources department, so I was the entire department. Actually I was the only employee in the whole company. Fortunately I had experience in the area of personnel, and that helped tremendously.

When I had been based out of Rome, working in marketing and sales for Eli Lilly, one day the vice president had called me into his office and asked me take over the human-resources department. I'd thought I'd misunderstood him. Outside of hiring a few people to work at my pharmacy in Amman years before, I'd had no experience in that area. I knew nothing about personnel and HR.

But when I expressed my doubts about the shift in jobs, the vice president assured me all I needed was good common sense. He sent me to Eli Lilly's headquarters in Indianapolis, Indiana, to receive basic training then told me to get busy organizing the department. Little did I know the year and a half I spent managing the company's human resources in Rome would turn out to be a highly valuable tool in helping me establish my personnel department at Hikma eventually.

I knew how well Eli Lilly took care of me, but heading up HR there gave me an opportunity to have a broader range of vision, to step up and look across the entire spectrum of the company and see just how well it took care of all its employees. It's one thing to work with your assigned boss, but when you're in the position of observing all the managers, seeing how they make and implement plans and policies, how they establish job positions as well as manage their employees, it's an education in itself.

The position gave me the experience I needed to evaluate employees' strengths then direct them to additional training so they could keep improving, which in turn fueled the corporation's growth. On top of that, I conducted salary surveys in the Middle East, which helped us stay competitive with what other pharmaceutical companies were paying their employees. And I learned all about employment laws as well as Eli Lilly's policies and benefits.

If you're going to start your own corporation, take the time to learn about human resources even if you're hiring experts to handle that department. The knowledge will be invaluable.

Hiring for Hikma

The best investment you can make is your employees.

I knew I needed to hire the highest-quality people I could find for Hikma because that was the only way I'd be able to manufacture the highest-quality pharmaceuticals. You can't turn out good products with inadequate employees.

But to hire the best, I'd have to pay good salaries to lure them away from my competitors. The problem was I didn't have a lot of money to spare. I couldn't afford to pay the highest salaries, but I did decide employees' paychecks would be in the top quarter of the current market, and those who worked for me would receive shares of the company's profits.

For years I'd been thinking about the qualities I wanted to see in my future Hikma employees. Finally I sat down one day and wrote out a list. Because I remembered how hard it had been to land a job when I'd first graduated from AUB, I was determined to give young talent a chance. Just because people don't have extensive work experience on their résumés, it doesn't mean they aren't viable. I was willing to consider all who came to me looking for jobs. If I thought they were good fits for the company, even if I didn't have positions available at that moment I would hire them anyway and find things for them to do somewhere.

I believe men and women should be given equal opportunities, and it shouldn't matter what nationalities or religions they are. In some countries, such as the United States, there are employment laws that forbid discrimination of any kind, but that's not the case in every country. It should be a given in any company in any country.

I didn't want to discriminate in any way, and I didn't want my employees to either. Regardless of who they were and what their positions were in the company, I decided to stress to all I hired that they had to respect their coworkers, not look down on them or treat them badly because of their positions or the beliefs they held. Plus I wanted my employees to know they had the right to speak up and voice their opinions respectfully.

I didn't want any kind of elitist atmosphere. We were going to be a team, all working together, so there weren't going to be any special perks like reserved parking spaces. No matter what your position, if you came to work early you'd get a prime spot near the door. There weren't going to be separate dining rooms for executives. Everyone would eat together in the cafeteria.

Potential job candidates had to have above-average intelligence with good scholastic records. They needed to show me they were optimistic, forward thinking, always looking for ways to improve themselves and the company. I wanted to see they were active in extracurricular activities such as sports or nonprofit organizations.

They had to have healthy self-esteem, but I didn't want arrogant personalities. Instead I wanted people who were very competent but modest about their achievements, not braggarts.

Above all I wanted to provide the right environment for growth and creativity. Employees are a company's greatest assets, and I wanted to be sure they not only were fulfilled in their careers but also enjoyed the work atmosphere at Hikma. I wanted to give all employees opportunities for additional training outside the company, but I wasn't going to guarantee they'd advance to higher positions if they weren't capable or if they didn't really have a desire to grow.

After writing out the blueprint for my ideal employees, I completed my plans for how I'd evaluate potential workers' strengths and weaknesses as well as the training programs they would need to complete in order to advance.

I had a few temporary, part-time workers, but I needed to start hiring full-time employees. Unfortunately, until the company was bringing in some money, I couldn't afford to go on a personnel shopping spree. However, I knew there was one critically important full-time position that would be the company's first hire: a maintenance technician to make sure all the machines on our production line remained in peak operating condition.

The person who filled that position would have to be intelligent and willing to learn new things and to work hard. That was exactly what I found in Ibrahim Shihadeh, a young, eager, single guy willing to put in long hours and excited about the prospect of growing with my fledgling company. He was my first hire. We were the only full-time permanent employees—and his paycheck was bigger than mine.

Neither one of us had a job title. We'd start the machines each morning, and I'd stand right next to him as we watched our brand-new pharmaceuticals moving along the production line. Hikma was our baby, and we gave it as much attention as any parents with their first newborn. As a team Ibrahim and I did whatever had to be done.

He hung in there with Hikma through all the growing pains. After a few years, Ibrahim found a lovely girl to marry and started a family, but he still continued to put in long hours. He even went into the plant on weekends to make sure everything was in order, his little boy Mohammad tagging along behind him, fascinated as he watched his daddy checking the electricity and the water. Mohammad was so cute and such a good little boy, I couldn't resist slipping him a few sweets each time I saw him.

Fortunately for me and for Hikma, my first employee was a very wise hire. Today Ibrahim is our senior director of MENA operations. His son, Mohammad, that cute little boy who learned the ins and outs of the company from a young age, decided Hikma was like a second home, and he wanted to stay. He obtained his bachelor's in chemistry and is now the purchasing supervisor for Hikma in Amman.

A few months after Ibrahim started working for me, in the spring of 1979, I was walking through the plant's cafeteria and noticed an older man I'd hired. He was eating a very meager lunch that consisted of only a thin slice of tomato and a chunk of dark bread. It stabbed me like a knife through the heart. I knew what it was like not to have enough money to eat well. I'd been there, and I remembered how awful it was.

I couldn't afford to give the man a raise at that point, but I knew I could feed him at least one decent meal each workday. We were already providing free tea to all our employees, but what good was that if they weren't getting enough to eat? Food was brainpower. If employees' stomachs were growling most of the day, and they weren't able to think clearly from a lack of nutrition, it wasn't good for them or the company.

Right then and there, I decided Hikma would provide free hot lunches for all our workers. Within two weeks the program was up and running. Today Hikma still provides free meals at all our factories.

Shortly after that I was attending a pharmaceutical association meeting when I heard a speaker there who really impressed me. I decided I wanted that man to work for Hikma.

Even though we were still small, with barely enough full-time staff to field two soccer teams, and were operating on only about US$500,000 a year, I knew I wanted to start exporting our products to the United States one day. I needed someone who not only knew the pharmaceutical business but could easily navigate the cultures of both the Middle East and America.

Dr. Ibrahim Jalal's credentials were impeccable—exactly what I was looking for. He was doing research at 3M's headquarters in Minnesota at the time, and his educational background was right on the mark. After obtaining his bachelor's from the University of Alexandria in Egypt, he'd moved to the United States to earn his master's in pharmaceutics at the University of the Sciences in Philadelphia and his doctorate, also in pharmaceutics, from the University of Wisconsin-Madison.

The day after I heard him lecture at the conference, I made Dr. Jalal a job offer.

Hikma, at that time, couldn't compete with the salaries the more-established pharmaceutical manufacturers were offering, but I promised him an innovative work environment and a total commitment to quality and research along with an opportunity to move up the ladder quickly.

Fortunately for us Dr. Jalal liked challenges. We had a new technical director.

Dr. Jalal is still with Hikma more than thirty-four years later. He's been our senior corporate vice president of technical affairs since 2008, and he was instrumental in helping Hikma achieve compliance with the US Food and Drug Administration (FDA) in order for us to begin manufacturing medications for shipment to the American market.

Another wise hire.

Give Young People Chances

Years in the business world, both in sales and personnel, have taught me to evaluate people with whom I come into contact carefully and constantly.

When my son, Said, attended high school in Beirut at International College, AUB's preparatory school, he was close friends with a boy named Ali Husry. Ali was a year ahead of him, but even after he graduated and went off to study mechanical engineering at the University of Southern California in Los Angeles, he stayed in touch with our family.

In the summer of 1978, after Ali had completed his third year at USC, he came to visit us in Amman. I realized I needed to recruit this talented and ambitious young man, so I asked him to join the company before it was even open for business. The plant was still under construction, and we were months away from being operational, but I didn't want another company to lure him away. Once I believe in a person, I'm willing to take a risk as long as he or she is willing to take on a challenge. Fortunately Ali recognized my offer as a great ground-floor opportunity.

Two years later, in early 1981, about seven months after Said and Ali had graduated, they both started working at Hikma. We had approximately eighty employees then, and our revenue was only about US$1 million. I still hadn't established any job titles. Instead we were a team, all working together—sometimes through trial and error—to get things done.

Ali and Said were fast learners, and I quickly realized both were showing strong leadership abilities. Because of Ali's background in mechanical engineering, I started him in the factory's maintenance department. When we began having productivity problems with the third graveyard shift because employees didn't have too much oversight and were slacking off a bit, I came up with a plan to solve that. Granted, working overnights can be difficult. Your body clock may not easily adjust to the flipped hours, and it's tempting not to push yourself as much if a supervisor isn't motivating you. But something had to be done to bring that shift in line with the other two.

I told Ali and Said the three of us would take turns working overnights in order to provide a little motivation for the workers. That's how much I trusted the two of them to get things done. As I expected, productivity improved greatly on that shift because the three of us kept things moving.

From the beginning I knew the two young men had great potential and were the future of Hikma, so I told Ali the same thing I told Said: "If you want to advance here, you have to get an MBA."

He and Said went to INSEAD together in 1984, and both graduated with master's degrees in business administration a year later.

When we decided to expand Hikma in 1989 and selected Portugal as the perfect location, I sent Ali to find a site to build a manufacturing plant there. He found a great property in Sintra, a suburb outside the capital, Lisbon, and negotiated the sale.

Ali's still with Hikma. He's been a member of the board since 2005.

Hikma Doesn't Rehire

We always try to find good fits between employees and job positions. As much as possible, Hikma tries to encourage a positive atmosphere of passion, skills, creativity, and intellect at each of our facilities. But sometimes workers just don't do well in anything or won't make efforts to get along with their coworkers. Sadly, sometimes we have to show those people the door. Fortunately, in more than thirty years of doing business, 95 percent of the people we've hired at Hikma have worked out.

We do have an exit policy at the company that we enforce: we won't rehire people we let go for whatever reason, and we won't rehire those who voluntarily leave.

For those employees who feel they need to quit and pursue what they consider better opportunities away from Hikma, we wish them well, but our exit policy is the door locks behind them. They aren't allowed to return. I've found that once someone loses the desire to work at Hikma, it's best for him or her and the company not to try to establish that relationship again.

Some corporate managers may not agree with that. True, it can cost half as much to rehire an ex-employee because he or she won't need the training time and expenses like a new hire does, but I've found problems crop up later. After some time away from their original jobs, people forget why they left in the first place. Suddenly they find the new jobs they thought would be better aren't, or they may start regretting the benefits they gave up at their old jobs. They get nostalgic for what they left behind. But as soon as they return to their old companies, too often the same issues crop up, and they're unhappy again. Why would you want to hire someone to go back to a job he or she had already decided once before he or she didn't want?

The Foundation Remains

Hikma's human-resources department still uses the hiring practices I wrote out more than thirty-five years ago. From one lone employee, we've grown into a workforce numbering more than seven thousand talented and diverse people. From one small manufacturing plant in Amman, Jordan, Hikma's grown to twelve factories in nine countries on four continents. In 1980 our revenue was US$1 million. Today it's more than US$1 billion.

When Hikma was just getting started, a lot of our employees agreed to work with us even though they were making less than they would have at more-established corporations. They hung in there with us as the company grew, and as soon as we became financially successful we rewarded them financially for their loyalty.

LESSON SIX

Treat Family Employees as Nonfamily

A round the world family businesses both small and large are the foundations of nations' economies. Most of those companies either have or will employ nonfamily at some point, as Hikma has from the beginning. With more than seven thousand employees worldwide, it's a safe bet all Hikma employees are *not* related to Samih Darwazah. I have only four children and eleven grandchildren. The Darwazah family would be pretty tired if we had to handle all the work those seven thousand employees do in all the countries around the globe where we have facilities. Not only that, but I can say without a doubt the corporation wouldn't have grown to be even a tenth of what it is today if I'd insisted on hiring only family members.

However, I absolutely admit my family was the number-one reason I founded Hikma. I wanted to provide a future for them, hopefully lasting many generations; I wanted to create something my children would be proud of, something that would not only improve their lives but be a place they wanted to work as much as I did.

I also imagined creating something larger than just my family. Even when Hikma was still on the drawing board, I was determined the company would eventually enrich the lives of my employees as well as my country and even the rest of the world.

Though I wanted my children to be an integral part of Hikma and to take over the reins of the company one day, I knew keeping a global corporation in the family isn't an easy task. Only one-third of family businesses survive long enough to make the transition to the second generation. Either the sons and daughters aren't interested in continuing the business, and they sell their controlling shares, or they make such drastic changes to the structure, products, and services they provide, it's almost impossible for the corporation to survive.

That meant my children had to have the same desire and passion for Hikma I did. As much as I wanted May, Said, Mazen, and Hana to work with me, I still wanted them to make that decision on their own.

When they were young, I gave them small tastes of what it was like for us to work together. When they were in their early teens, I would occasionally let them come with me to my offices at Eli Lilly so they could see what I did. They were fascinated by the different types of printed promotional materials we gave to medical professionals showing the quality of our products.

To help them feel more connected to my career, I had them help me stuff envelopes. We'd customize letters with doctors' names then insert each one in an envelope and address the outside. They earned one cent for each letter and even competed with each other to see who could earn the most.

But when the four of them were choosing their careers, Samira and I always encouraged them to think about what their interests were first. If they worked for me only because they were trying to please me, and their hearts weren't in it, it wouldn't really benefit them, me, their coworkers, or the company. They had to have a passion for Hikma just as I did—the same thing I expect of all my employees. I knew they would need that passion to weather any storms the company might face in the future. They had to *want* to be there. I didn't push any of them to join Hikma. If they wanted others careers or to work for other companies, that was fine. My work was my passion, not just a means to a paycheck, and Samira and I always impressed upon them the importance of doing what they love.

Do what you enjoy, and you'll be excellent because you like what you're doing.

I've learned from experience that if you see something you know is good and worthwhile, you shouldn't hesitate to go after it and grab it. Spend what you need to obtain it. Go through the hard times, and pay your dues. Things may get tough, and money may be tight, but if you believe in something strongly enough you'll find a way to make everything work out. Your passion will see you through.

Good things are worth waiting for. I guarantee you'll have to wait because no new business will show a profit right away. That was certainly true of mine. I have to admit my faith wavered in the two years prior to Hikma's official opening. Banks wouldn't help me, and I was almost penniless by the time the first factory was completed. I wondered if I'd made the wrong decision when I'd walked away from a steady paycheck and opted for the uncertainty of being an entrepreneur. But I rode out the storm, and things got better. I needed to know my children and grandchildren would be equally committed to Hikma, to be able to ride out the storms that would come when they were in control of the company.

As it turns out, all four of my children have affinities for pharmaceutical manufacturing and its end result of saving lives. Perhaps my enthusiasm helped inspire them. Fortunately for me and for Hikma, all four decided they wanted to be part of the company. Though I'm overjoyed to see my children and now some of their children choose to work for our organization, I find it interesting none of them chose my first profession, pharmacy, and Hana's the only one of the four who briefly chose Samira's profession—teaching.

Once my children had declared they were interested in working with me at the company, I had to figure out how to merge my family and nonfamily one day in an equal way. Then I had to figure out how to set the foundation for Hikma to survive beyond the tenure of the founding employees not only for my family but also for the family members of my employees who would want to follow in their footsteps too.

It can be delicate merging family and nonfamily employees, especially if nonfamily feel they're losing promotions to the owner's family. Though I dearly love my children and grandchildren and have always wanted them to be part of the company, I also love my employees as if they were my family. I've never wanted any Hikma workers to feel inferior in any way, and that policy of equality continues today.

My wife, my children, and I are a tight-knit family, but being close at home doesn't always translate into working well together in the business world. I knew nobody would be as committed to Hikma as my children, but I had to insist on certain working relationships; otherwise there could be a lack of professionalism and accountability.

Long ago I determined family members would not receive preferential treatment at Hikma. They had to apply for positions and work hard just like everyone else. They had to earn their promotions and raises, advance in education, and learn further skills the same as the rest of my employees.

May, Said, Mazen, and Hana started on the bottom rung of Hikma's corporate ladder, which for each of them was actually a physical ladder in the warehouse. They unpacked shipments and stocked the shelves going up and down that ladder.

Like all Hikma employees, my children had to prove themselves in different departments and capacities before getting promotions. All four worked their ways up through the company, but their starting jobs and salaries were at the bottom.

Mazen likes to remind me his first position at the company paid less in a month than his rent cost. Of course the positive in that is all four learned to appreciate better the free room and board Dad and Mom provided them while they were growing up.

When the company started, all my employees were nonfamily members. But within a few years, as my children began graduating from college, they joined Hikma. Now my grandchildren are joining the company, and they've all been wonderful additions, contributing much to the smooth running and profit of the corporation.

My sons and daughters are all humble despite their many accomplishments, and they've raised their children the same way. Many of my grandchildren didn't realize until they were in their late teens that their family owns a billion-dollar company.

In previous chapters I introduced you to some of Hikma's employees. Now allow me to introduce you to my children and grandchildren.

May Darwazah Murad

Our eldest child, May, was the first to reach college age. She decided she wanted to return to the United States for her university years, one reason being that she'd loved the two years we'd spent in America when I was getting my master's in Missouri and my first year with Eli Lilly at their headquarters in Indiana. After we'd moved from St. Louis, we'd rented a three-bedroom house in the Indianapolis suburbs for a year, and May had become very familiar with the area.

So it was really no surprise to Samira and me that when it came time to select a college, May chose one that was not only academically tops but in an area near our former home. Because she'd always liked the people of Indiana (they are some of the friendliest and most helpful people we've ever met), she selected Purdue University in West Lafayette, less than an hour's drive northwest of Indianapolis.

May majored in finance and management and, after graduating with a bachelor of science degree, helped me establish Orient Traders, a medical-equipment import company.

A few years later, in 1979, she married Mansour Murad, an ambitious, young mechanical engineer. Mansour now owns his own business, which focuses on implementing green energy in Jordan and the Middle East.

May and Mansour lived in Saudi Arabia for a few years early in their marriage, but when they decided to return to Jordan, May fortunately opted to come share her talents with Hikma. I put her skills to good use in the purchasing and planning department as well as with over-the-counter (OTC) products.

May's always been very artistic and interested in construction and remodeling. So after working for Hikma for a number of years, she made the decision to leave the company and begin renovating houses, utilizing her talents in architecture and interiors.

May's daughter, Zeena, was our first grandchild. Because she's the oldest of that third generation, she puts enormous pressure on herself to act professional and responsible at all times. But when she was a teenager, she put too much pressure on herself to look perfect. She's a stunning girl, and I'm not saying that just because she's my granddaughter. Zeena is strikingly beautiful. But for some reason when she was younger, she decided she was too heavy and needed to lose weight. Between fashion magazines and television, many teenagers believe they need to look practically like skeletons.

Zeena's desire to shed some pounds coincided with my own desire to lose weight. I'd started using some natural weight-loss supplements, which I stored in the refrigerator. One day I caught her reading the ingredients list on the bottle.

I told her she didn't need those pills to lose weight because she was young and healthy. She reluctantly put them back in the refrigerator and promised not to use them, but I guess the temptation was too great, and her desire to look model skinny was too compelling. A few days later, Zeena and her mother were eating dinner with us when Zeena suddenly grabbed her stomach and doubled over. We were all concerned, but then I happened to remember her fascination with my diet pills.

Old habits stay with you. My years of being a pharmacist and counting pills were still with me. When I checked the bottle of diet supplements, I could tell one or two pills were missing—an amount too small to hurt her but enough to cause her some discomfort. After drinking herbal tea, Zeena started feeling better. Later she came to me, tears in her eyes, and confessed she'd secretly taken the pills.

"I'm sorry, Granddad," she sniffed. "I just wanted to try them."

One thing I've always told my children and grandchildren is if you feel ashamed of something, don't do it. By the same token, if you feel convicted enough to do something, then own it, and don't be ashamed of it.

Zeena learned her lesson. She's incredibly smart, but even smart people make mistakes.

She went on to earn her bachelor's degree at the University of London's Royal Holloway then got her master's in investment management. After working for a European bank for several years, she expressed an interest in working for Hikma and moved to our London office, where she's now our investor-relations manager. Zeena's a huge asset to our company—a total professional and a bit of a workaholic. She's driven to succeed and sets enormously high goals then pushes herself to accomplish them in the shortest amount of time.

She charges through life the same way she plows through her work responsibilities and is one of my most adventurous grandchildren—a bit of a courageous daredevil. I was horrified when one day she excitedly told me she'd gone skydiving.

"It was amazing! Unbelievable!" she gushed.

"You mean you jumped out of an airplane?" I gasped.

"Granddad, I did have a parachute," she said, a mischievous look in her eyes.

I couldn't believe she'd paid good money to plunge out of a perfectly stable airplane, but I'm always glad to see my grandchildren trying new things and, at times, pushing the boundaries of safe and secure.

May's number-two daughter, Deema, is an amazing artist and designer. One of her beautiful paintings hangs in a place of honor in my home; it's the first thing everyone sees when they come in. The artwork is so good, they always wants to know more about the artist, which, of course, makes us incredibly proud.

Deema's always been interested in mechanical engineering too, just like her father. After getting her bachelor's in graphic design at the University of Reading in Berkshire, England, she decided to go from two dimensional to 3-D and got her master's in industrial and product design at Central Saint Martins University of the

Arts in London. While she was there, she built a prototype of a self-energizing, dual-powered, full-suspension tricycle and even obtained a US patent on the design. I liked her invention so much, I decided to sponsor her.

In 2012 Deema married a wonderful young man named Maher Bseiso. They now live in Kuwait, where Deema works as a creative director specializing in branding. She's also starting a marketing department at Hikma Kuwait.

Omar is May's youngest child. During his summer vacations when he was in high school, he worked part time at Hikma Jordan, stocking inventory in our warehouse for products and packaging materials. Because May was in Hikma's purchasing department, the other workers used to tease Omar that he was carrying all the boxes of products his mother had ordered.

Omar, just like his older sister and his father, had an early fascination with all things mechanical and was always trying to find someone who would let him drive the lorry palette in the warehouse. He was far too young—one reason why no one would give him permission—but we had to give him credit for his persistence.

Unfortunately Omar's fascination with mechanical things became a bit too obsessive. When he was sixteen, he made the decidedly unwise decision not to tell anyone he was taking a joy-ride in my brand-new car. Naturally my first thought was that my car had been stolen, but May knew her son and his passion all too well and had a suspicion he might be driving it. However, when she called Omar on his cell phone, he denied having the car.

Bad decision.

I went ahead and called the police to report my car had been stolen.

Omar quickly drove back to my house, figuring he was in big trouble. He knew I'd be angry because I'd know he'd lied as soon as I saw him drive up. So when he got back to my house and saw the police there, he decided the better option was to turn himself in to them rather than face my wrath.

Smart boy.

Kids.

Omar finally channeled his fascination with mechanics into a career. After earning his bachelor's in civil and energy engineering from the University of Birmingham in England, he started working with Mansour as an energy analyst.

In September 2013 Omar started working at Hikma in the engineering department, applying his expertise in energy efficiency to pharmaceutical production. His energy program at Hikma has already made a positive impact, and he continues to hone his skills in industrial engineering.

Said Darwazah

My older son, Said, who is four years younger than May, followed in his big sister's footsteps and selected Purdue University for his undergraduate degree. What can I say? My children really liked Indiana.

Said and his then-girlfriend (now wife) Mariana "Mami" Melhem, who was also a student at Purdue, were so familiar with American culture they knew how to score buy-one-get-one-free buckets of chicken at the Kentucky Fried Chicken near campus. Their tip? Show up just before closing time, when KFC was slashing prices to get rid of what was left at the end of the day.

Said graduated with his bachelor of science degree in industrial engineering in 1980. (In 2011 Purdue and its alumni organization selected him to receive their outstanding industrial engineer award.) Fortunately for us, after graduating, Said decided to come back to Amman to work for Hikma.

I assigned him to several different departments so he could be exposed to and gain experience in all aspects of the company, including working as a salesman promoting our products to physicians around the Middle East. More than two years later, I asked him if he saw himself running Hikma in the future. When he said he did, I asked him if he knew the degrees our top managers had.

"Most of them have master's degrees. Some are PhDs," he said.

"Well, if you expect to run this company someday, you're going to have to get an MBA," I said. "That's the very least I'll accept from you. Otherwise there will be more-qualified candidates."

He didn't seem too thrilled about going back to college, but I knew he had wonderful abilities still hidden that he wasn't challenging himself enough to explore—skills only a formal classroom setting would bring out. Sometimes a parent needs to give a child a dose of medicine for his own good even if he doesn't want it.

I'd started my company for my family, and I wanted it to stay in the family as long as possible, but I wasn't going to give anyone a free ride to the top even if that person was my son. If Said were going to run my company one day—and I really did want him to be the one to take over that position from me—I had to insist he get his MBA.

"If you want to make your way up in this company, you're going to have to work for it like everyone else," I said. "You have to go back to school."

I told Said I wanted him to attend one of the best business schools in the world—INSEAD. Within a year he had earned his master's degree in business administration.

When he returned to Jordan in 1985, I appointed him head of the marketing department. Six years later he was instrumental in Hikma's acquiring our first American-based facility: West-Ward Pharmaceuticals in New Jersey, a company he headed for three years as president and CEO, beginning in 1991. During that time he was key in helping Hikma's facilities in New Jersey gain FDA approval.

In 1994 I brought him back to Jordan to take over my office as chairman and CEO of Hikma. He was instrumental in helping our facilities in Portugal and Jordan gain FDA approval, just as he'd done with our facility in New Jersey, and was key to developing our injectables business in Europe and the MENA region.

He was running Hikma so well, he made the radar of King Abdullah II and other government officials. I stepped back in and assumed those positions at Hikma in 2003, when Said was tapped for a cabinet position in Jordan's government serving as minister of health, a position he held for four years.

In 2007 Said returned to Hikma as CEO and became executive director of the board. He still holds those positions as I write this in 2013. The company's already been passed to the second generation exactly as I'd hoped.

Said's excellent at acquiring companies that focus on innovative ideas, something that has helped take Hikma and the pharmaceutical industry in new directions. He's passionate about promoting better health care, which I love to see. He founded and is chairman of Jordan's Health Care Accreditation Council, a nonprofit organization that helps improve health care and accredits providers in the industry. He's also a director on the board of Endeavour Jordan, a nonprofit that helps nurture entrepreneurs.

Said and Mami have four children: my namesake, Samih; Kareem; Yasmine; and Shareef, the youngest of my eleven grandchildren. He is still in high school in Jordan.

Because Said and his family often travel to different countries on business trips and vacations, he, Mami, and their children are used to eating at some of the finest restaurants in the world.

Enter Granddad with a dose of reality.

When Samih, a sweet, young man with mild Down syndrome who's currently in school in the United States, and his brother, Shareef, are both in Jordan, they love having lunch with me at a local street vendor's hot-dog stand. I want them to see that even though it's nice to eat in world-class restaurants, they can still enjoy simpler things.

No matter how high they rise socially and professionally, I want each of my children and grandchildren to keep a humble and down-to-earth attitude, never taking things for granted.

Said's and Mami's son, Kareem, interned for two summers in our injectables divisions in Portugal and Amman. One day I overheard him asking one of our employees what kind of glass cleaner we used on our windows. I love the fact that he's curious and notices a lot of the little but still important details.

Kareem's now studying at my alma mater, American University of Beirut, and his younger sister, Yasmine, is in Wellesley, Massachusetts, just outside Boston, attending Babson College—one of the top schools for those who want to study entrepreneurship.

Mazen Darwazah

Our third child, Mazen, went to high school in Lebanon and grew to love the country so much, he decided to remain there for his university years. He earned his bachelor's in business administration from the Lebanese American University in Beirut and now serves on the college's board of international advisors.

While he was attending LAU, he met Rula Naser, a beautiful Jordanian girl who was studying economics at the nearby American University of Beirut. They married a few years later.

Mazen started as a medical rep at Hikma in 1985, when he was twenty-seven. He went to INSEAD as his older brother Said had but instead of the MBA program chose to go through the intensive advanced management program.

Mazen's held various positions, including chairman and CEO of Hikma Pharmaceuticals Limited, our major group operational and holding company. He's been executive vice chairman of Hikma and CEO of our MENA operations since 2005.

Since Mazen's so good at establishing relationships with high-caliber people in government, politics, and business, he's our go-to guy both for smoothing out any issues Hikma might run into with governments and for building relationships with current or potential licensors of our pharmaceuticals. He also keeps Hikma focused on maintaining ethical behavior in everything we do and heads up our corporate social-responsibility and business-integrity programs.

In addition to his responsibilities at Hikma, Mazen serves the nation of Jordan as a senator, a position he's held since 2010.

Mazen's and Rula's older son (and my oldest grandson), Tareq, started doing summer internships at Hikma then went on Marquette University in Milwaukee, Wisconsin, where he earned his bachelor's degree. He started working for Hikma as a sales rep based out of our Jordan facility then, a few years later, went back to school and earned his master's in public policy focusing on health care at the University of Chicago. Tareq's now special-projects manager at West-Ward Pharmaceutical, Hikma's manufacturing facility in Eatontown, New Jersey.

Tareq's younger brother, Walid, also worked at our Jordan facility during his summer breaks from school. When he told me he was choosing business management as his college major because he loved it so much, I was glad to hear he wasn't in it just for the money. If he'd told me all he cared about was how much he could make, I would have told him to find something else because he wouldn't become a success with that kind of thinking. In 2011 he earned his bachelor's from Babson College in Massachusetts—the same school his cousin, Yasmine, later selected.

When Walid's friend asked him if he was going to work for Hikma after graduation, he said he wanted to and was definitely going to apply, but he didn't know if he'd be hired. Just because he was a Darwazah didn't mean it was a done deal.

I'm glad my grandchildren realize there are no entitlements at Hikma whether you're a second-generation Darwazah or the second generation of any employee working with us (and we do have second-generation nonfamily employees). If you're hired it's because your education and/or job experience qualifies you for the position no matter who you are. There is no preferential treatment at our company. My grandchildren know this going in. They know they can't use their lineage or family privilege to help them advance in their careers.

Arrogance is the one thing that could destroy our company. Thankfully there's no trace of it in the third generation of the family business. When I look at my grandchildren, I see humility and willingness to work—and that gives me hope for the future.

Walid did apply to Hikma after graduating from Babson. We had a position available matching his education and qualifications—and we hired him.

Hana Darwazah Ramadan

When it comes to communication, our number-two daughter and youngest child, Hana, is the expert. She was the first in our family to master English at the ripe old age of three, and she's been off and running with it ever since. She has used her language skills well during her career, first as a writer and an editor for a research center in Jordan then later as an English-language business instructor.

She's always had a passion for teaching, much like her parents. That's probably one reason (of many) she was attracted to Omar Ramadan, a pilot and flight engineer who's also a certified flight instructor. They married in 1988.

Hana graduated with a bachelor's in international studies from the American College of Switzerland then got her MBA specializing in organizational psychology and development from American Intercontinental University.

Fortunately for us she brought her great communication skills to Hikma when she came to work for us in 2001. Hana's now vice president of our corporate communications department and heads up our corporate social responsibility department, which she established.

She's also been an enormous help to me in putting together not only this book but my previous one as well.

Hana and her older sister, May, are wonderful role models for their daughters and all women. They've shown how powerful women can become when they're allowed to use their educations and skills to reach their potential and rise in the corporate world.

Hana's and Omar's older daughter, Tamara, obtained her bachelor's in public administration from my alma mater,

American University of Beirut. As I write this, she's in London with me, putting her career on hold for a short time while she helps me finish this book. Together we're also working to establish a foundation that focuses on education and women's rights in the Middle East. Hopefully our efforts will help improve lives and communities for many years to come.

Tamara's younger sister, Natasha, has always been artistic and is currently studying visual-arts communication in the United States at the School of the Art Institute of Chicago in Illinois.

The New Generation

At Hikma our faith in the new generation is without limits with both our family and our employees' children. We want them to feel that same sense of opportunity and know that what they can achieve with us depends entirely on their own efforts and ambition. There have never been any ceilings or limits at Hikma. If there were how could I ever have had the goal of creating the first Arab-owned multinational company? It had never been done before, but that didn't mean I wasn't going to try.

Since my grandchildren have started working at Hikma, I've always impressed upon them that the company is for them and their children as well as for our employees and their children. They can't be in it to make a quick buck and get out but instead have to make greater commitments to our coworkers, our customers, and the communities we serve.

All my grandchildren have been encouraged to ask questions and form their own opinions but always to back up those opinions with reason followed by action. That's how to develop critical and analytical thinking skills. Every issue should be considered from different, multidimensional perspectives—the only way to arrive at a more complete picture.

My grandchildren have never seen their parents take shortcuts or expect any kind of special treatment in Hikma based on their last name. My children had to earn advanced degrees in order to receive promotions in the company. I always insisted all my top management members have solid educations, and my children and grandchildren are no exceptions. In fact they may have had it a little harder. I never asked other executives why they brought home a B instead of an A.

Personal and professional values should always be in alignment. You should be the same person whether you're sitting at your desk, a conference-room table, or your own dining-room table. I've always told my children to calculate the risks of whatever they're planning to do and think about the probabilities of success. However, the risks are much greater now. The only thing I lost when I started my own company was a job at Eli Lilly, but my grandchildren will be risking far more because the future of an entire multinational corporation will be resting on their shoulders. That's a lot of responsibility, caring for the futures and well being of thousands of employees and the families they support.

But I want this generation to see there are no limitations to what they can achieve. It doesn't matter where they come from or where they put down roots. The important thing is for them to keep learning and growing.

Know How and When to Expand Sales Internationally

As I raced through the night in a desperate attempt to save my children, I thought about how one gunshot more than two thousand miles away could have impacted my life in such a profound way.

Three days earlier Israel's ambassador to Britain had been shot. It turned out to be yet another "shot heard round the world," as Ralph Waldo Emerson famously said about the start of the American Revolutionary War in his poem "Concord Hymn."

As Israeli ambassador Shlomo Argov had been getting into a car in London, gunmen linked to a Palestinian named Abu Nidal had put a bullet through his head. That shot on June 3, 1982, definitely was heard throughout the Middle East.

Israeli defense minister Ariel Sharon accused Yasser Arafat and his Palestinian Liberation Organization of being behind the ambassador's assassination attempt (the gunshot did not kill him). The PLO claimed they were innocent, that Abu Nidal was a rogue agent who wanted to kill their people, and that Iraq's Saddam Hussein had funded Nidal because they were trying to start a new war between Israel and the PLO.

If so, they got their wish.

The next day Israel bombed PLO ammo depots in Lebanon. Arafat and the PLO had set up camp in Southern Lebanon in 1971 after being driven out of Jordan for trying to kill King Hussein and take over the Hashemite Kingdom. For years the PLO and Israel had been trading gunfire and missiles across the Lebanon-Israel border. The assassination attempt on the ambassador proved to be the excuse Israel was looking for to justify wiping out as many of the PLO fighters as they could.

In retaliation for Israel's bombing of Southern Lebanon, the PLO fired Katyusha rockets into Israel. Two days later, on June 6, Israeli troops crossed the border into Lebanon determined to push Arafat and his forces at least twenty-five miles north, beyond Beirut, to create a buffer zone.

It was all-out war.

And my children were trapped in the middle of it.

The assassination attempt on the ambassador left him in a coma for three months and paralyzed for the remaining twenty-one years of his life, and it led to the deaths of more than twelve thousand people; some say it was as many as eighteen thousand. It also set off another round of revenge and counter-revenge between Israel and the PLO.

I'd been keeping a careful eye on events as they were unfolding, and once I learned Israeli troops had crossed the border into Lebanon, I knew I had to act quickly. My two youngest children, Mazen and Hana, were in school in Beirut. I had to get to them before the fighting escalated.

Leaving Samira at our home in Amman, I jumped into my car and sped north into Syria, careful to stay within its borders as long as possible before turning west toward Beirut. No flights were going into or out of Beirut's Rafic Hariri International Airport, so I knew my only chance to reach Mazen and Hana would be by car. I was fighting panic while recalling previous wars I'd been through, including one in April 1975 when Samira, our children, and I had been forced to flee Beirut. Lebanon, unfortunately, had been a battleground for years with the players constantly changing and even switching alliances.

Lebanon's Christian Maronites, Druze community, and Shias in the southern part of the country supported Israel and wanted Arafat and his supporters out because PLO members were trying to take over the government there the same way they'd tried to in Jordan. Later, the Lebanese turned against Israel.

Did I fail to mention the Syrians were involved? Their military forces had entered Lebanon in 1976 saying they wanted to protect Christians and conservative Muslims from the PLO. Then the

Syrians joined forces with the PLO against Israel after the Israelis shot down more than eighty Syrian planes and destroyed the Soviet-designed anti-aircraft missile system that was supposed to protect Syria—all within the first few days of the invasion. Eventually the Lebanese turned against the Syrian military and demanded they leave their country too.

Welcome to the Middle East, where every war requires a scorecard to keep straight who's trying to kill whom.

It takes a hearty corporation to be able to survive events like that. Unfortunately, a year earlier, Hikma had expanded for the first time out of Jordan with exports into Lebanon. How's that for luck? I really knew how to pick an export market, didn't I?

War was about to take a nasty bite out of my young business, but at that moment I was more concerned with finding my two children and getting them out of harm's way as well as making sure my Lebanese medical reps were safe.

I got to Hana's school first. She was scared but didn't want to leave. Exercising my parental authority, I told her in no uncertain terms she was overruled and to pack her belongings quickly because we were leaving.

I couldn't reach Mazen, but he'd left word he was planning to escape on a boat, fleeing across the Mediterranean for the island of Cyprus, about 150 miles northwest of Beirut. At Larnaca International, Cyprus's main airport, he finally managed to get a flight home to Amman.

It's a good thing we all got out when we did. Fewer than forty-eight hours after we'd fled Beirut, Israelis surrounded the city. If I'd waited any longer, either I wouldn't have been able to reach Hana, or we wouldn't have been able to escape from the city. Within days Israeli forces moved to seal off the Syria-Lebanon border—the same border I'd crossed—and sever the Beirut-Damascus highway I'd just driven. The Syrians blocked the Israelis just three miles south of the highway and engaged in some heavy fighting. We would have been trapped right in the middle of a war zone.

My children were safe, but Lebanon wasn't.

Arafat was headquartered in Beirut, and in an attempt to drive him out, Israelis began shelling the city, destroying more than five hundred buildings within weeks. The once-beautiful Beirut where my family and I had lived was now mainly rubble.

Terrified residents who had remained in the city had no electricity and no way to get fresh supplies of water or food. Concerned about the civilians who were caught in the crossfire, US president Ronald Reagan publicly protested the Beirut bombings, a pressure play that caused Israel's government to strip Defense Minister Ariel Sharon of most of his powers.

For seven weeks the Israelis tightened their hold around Beirut, bombing the city continuously, unwilling to enter and engage in hand-to-hand combat with the PLO for fear of even-higher casualties among their own troops.

Finally, after a UN- and US-brokered cease-fire agreement, Arafat and his forces fled Beirut by ship to Greece and set up their new headquarters in Tunisia. The agreement also provided a way for the more than two thousand Syrian troops holed up in the Lebanese capital to flee.

On August 23 Israeli forces entered Beirut. I realized within the first few days of the war that I had to pull the plug on Hikma's export business into Lebanon. We couldn't ship supplies into the country, and our medical reps couldn't safely travel to meet with our customers. No amount of money was worth putting them in harm's way. I pulled Hikma out of Lebanon, losing a large part of our investment.

So much for my first international export market.

Expanding Beyond Jordan

When I'd started Hikma, my goal had been first to market and sell our pharmaceutical products within our home country of Jordan, but, coming from a large global corporation like Eli Lilly, I always knew we would expand internationally. Jordan's not a large place. We could sell only so many pharmaceutical products there.

I knew if Hikma were ever going to grow, we had to expand into other countries.

Once I knew our manufacturing facility in Amman was running well, that our products were excellent quality, and that our Hikma employees were well prepared for growth, I moved ahead with the next phase: exporting our products from Jordan.

Taking your business across borders involves some planning. I knew it meant we would be dealing with regulatory laws within Jordan concerning shipping medications out of the country as well as similar governmental import and licensing laws in foreign countries. We had to consider how we were going to handle and manage sales, foreign currency, and distribution. Would it be a problem taking money out of a foreign country? Some nations insist you keep the majority of your profits from sales within their borders. What about foreign tax laws and insurance?

I chose Lebanon as Hikma's first export market for several reasons. For one, it happened to be the fastest-growing market for pharmaceuticals in the Middle East. Even though it's a small country, it was the first in the region to offer Social Security and health insurance to its people, a move that helped the medical profession and the pharmaceutical market expand.

Another reason I selected Lebanon was I knew the country very well. I was familiar with the culture and the people not only because I'd gone to college in Beirut but because I'd lived there and worked in the pharmaceutical industry when I'd been with Eli Lilly. I knew the distribution channels well and still kept in touch with a lot of former colleagues and acquaintances in the Lebanon medical community.

That's certainly the first thing to consider when planning to export. If you can pick a country you know well, where you have a lot of friends and business contacts, you'll have people who can help you navigate more easily the pitfalls that come with expansion on foreign soil. And trust me, there will be pitfalls. Always have a plan B ready for when things go wrong—like war.

In 1981, a year before the Israel-Lebanon war started, I

traveled to Beirut and met with the necessary government officials, securing the license required for exporting pharmaceutical products into their country. I then quickly arranged for a Lebanese distributor as well as a few representatives to make sales calls.

We got off to great start. Our products were selling quite well until the war began. But I knew I couldn't afford to wait around for that closed and locked door to open. I didn't know how long it would be before normal business could resume in Lebanon. I quickly had to find an available export market that would provide Hikma an easy entry.

Indonesia and Malaysia came to mind because they were Muslim countries. Thailand seemed like a good location for expansion too, but our feasibility studies and research quickly revealed those Far Eastern markets wouldn't be that profitable for us. All three countries were interested only in cheap pharmaceuticals, and local companies there were already manufacturing those. We were selling generic drugs, which cost much less than name-brand medications, but pharmaceutical companies in the Far East were supplying drugs that were even cheaper than generics. There was no way for us to compete and make any kind of a profit.

I went back to my research, trying to find the best export markets for our Hikma products.

Planning International Expansion

So, what's your strategy for international expansion?

Certainly a basic consideration is making sure your company is prepared both financially and with support services and personnel, but there are some other foundational areas you need to make sure are sufficiently covered.

When I first started expanding Hikma, personal computers and the Internet were still in their infancy. But today, don't even consider moving forward internationally (even on the domestic front) unless you have a well-designed corporate website up and running as well as staff who can answer any e-mails or phone calls from your potential customers.

The first thing a potential client will do is check out your Internet presence then check to see if there are any complaints about your firm on other sites. Take the time and pay the money to make sure your website is current and attractive. Hire an expert webmaster as well as a skilled graphic designer and a writer to guarantee you're presenting the best-possible public image. Make sure your site is user friendly with easy-to-access tabs indicating all areas of your business people want to view.

If your website is poorly designed with grammatical errors, that tells potential clients you don't care about your business too much, so why should they?

I can't stress this enough: a well-designed website lends an air of credibility to your corporation the same way well-designed promotional materials and packaging do.

Another thing to consider is who your competition will be in a new international market. You may be the king of the pack in your headquarters country, but that will probably change once you enter a new market. Do your research, and make sure you're prepared to go head to head with those other firms.

The World Bank is a good place to start your research. Employees there can offer detailed background information about a country's economy, infrastructure, and politics. The Internet, of course, is an excellent research tool. And don't forget to check out the official government website of the country where you're hoping to export.

Make sure your managers are all onboard with the expansion and are prepared to handle the additional work and sales. Ask yourself what will happen to your firm if you don't expand much in a new market. Now ask what will happen if your company expands too quickly. Will your supply be able to keep up with the new, urgent demand? The worse thing would be if you failed to meet your orders or, even worse, skimped on quality in a rush to fulfill them. Make sure you're prepared.

Another thing to consider is your price point. You're going to have additional costs going into a foreign country, like travel and shipping. Make sure your products aren't priced too high to sell, but they also shouldn't be so low you're not making a profit. Carefully tally up *all* the costs associated with your new expansion, and don't forget to take into consideration the always-fluctuating currency-exchange rates. Is the country where you're planning to expand experiencing out-of-control inflation? That's going to hit your profit margins.

How do you plan to transport your products? Is your financing in place? Are your investors and your bank onboard with your exporting to new markets? Do you have a line of credit if you need to access it quickly?

Are you familiar with the culture of the country into which you're expanding? When Hikma expanded into countries where the populations were predominantly Muslim, we couldn't sell products that had any alcohol in them. That meant we had to change some of our ingredients without affecting the quality of the medications. Do your homework.

Do you have emergency support in your new export market if anything should go wrong or if there's a civil uprising in that country? Will your employees be safe? Don't forget always to check in with your own country's embassy when traveling internationally. They can help you through a lot of difficult situations.

What are the employment labor laws in the new country? Even if sweatshops are acceptable to that government, is your firm going to come under fire from activists or the press once they discover you're associated with less-than-ideal circumstances for your employees? Make sure your public-relations team is always prepared to answer questions from journalists carefully and diplomatically because even a few days of bad press can kill your sales practically overnight.

We make sure Hikma employees always behave as good citizens in every community where we work. We stick with our work ethic as well as our standards and core values of quality, but we always respect our host countries' customs and ideals. Your company's expansion should never feel like an enemy invasion.

Still, we try to use as few expatriate employees as possible. Workers from the country where you're expanding know the area and customs better than any foreigner. Besides, it can be expensive and psychologically difficult for someone other than top management to adjust to living abroad.

Do you need to hire a lawyer in your new export market, or are your own attorneys in your home country versed well enough in international law to handle any legal issues? How sure are you you'll receive payment for your products from your new clients? If you're dealing directly with a foreign government, are you prepared to wait for upward of a year to receive payment? Will you be able to survive until their checks come through? If you don't get paid, how do you plan to handle debt collection in a foreign country?

Find mentors who have paved the way before you. Don't be too proud to ask for their advice. Some governments even have agencies staffed with experienced businesspeople who can help you avoid some of the pitfalls before you run into trouble.

Don't go global until you're really ready, but remember you're not only growing your business; you're also providing a service and jobs to the citizens of another country. Make sure your corporation creates as many opportunities for those citizens as possible.

A Word Isn't Always What You Think It Is

One important area to take into consideration when you're naming your company or products or even putting together marketing materials is the differences between languages. To make sure you don't accidentally offend some of your international customers, early in your naming process you should bring onboard skilled linguists who are familiar with the areas where you're considering expansion.

Hikma products are sold in dozens of countries on five different continents, so we have to be careful with the way our advertising and literature are translated into the local languages. Some words have different meanings even in the same language.

For example, the Arabic word *afia* means "health" in Jordan, but in Tunisia it means "hell." Obviously we don't want to tell our Tunisian customers to go to hell, so we have to find another way to wish them good health.

Just because people speak the same language, it doesn't mean they're speaking the same language. That's not even taking into consideration how a successful product name in one country can be a complete disaster in another country where words mean the opposite of what you intend.

The best thing is to bring in an experienced and very qualified linguistic team early in the naming process so you can find neutral terms that won't offend your international customers. That's what Procter & Gamble did when they chose the name Dreft for one of their soap products. So did Kodak when they selected their company's name.

It's certainly easier and more cost effective if you're able to use the same brand name in many different international markets, but in some instances you may need to change the name to make sure your sales aren't affected adversely.

In our case we had to find a new name for our company in order to gain access to one Middle Eastern country. I'd named my company Life Pharma when we'd started, but that was too English-sounding for Saudi Arabia's government officials. They wouldn't even consider allowing our products into their country unless we had an Arabic name.

Fortunately we were still a young company, so a name change wasn't too detrimental to our sales. On March 20, 1982, we officially became Hikma Pharmaceuticals. *Hikma* in Arabic means "wisdom" or "reason," from *al hakim*, the word for a poet, philosopher, or wise man. Many pharmacists were also known as al hakim, so the name made for a good corporate identity.

That was the first hurdle to gaining access to the Saudi Arabian market. There were more-difficult obstacles to conquer before we could begin exporting to Saudis.

Finding New International Sales Markets

When you're just starting out, you have to go slowly unless you're independently wealthy or you've been blessed with extremely wealthy investors.

I didn't fit into either of those categories. I had investors, but they weren't that wealthy.

In my search for a new export market, I once again considered the Middle East. After all it was my home region, and I knew it well. Even though it was constantly dealing with wars, there had to be someplace that needed our products.

My eventual goal was to reach the large, lucrative markets in the United States and Europe, but Hikma was still young, and we didn't have the financial resources to expand into those areas just yet. As I looked around my own MENA region, I started reconsidering Syria. It was right next door to Jordan, so it seemed the most logical.

The doors opened, and Syria became our second foreign market followed by Iraq, Bahrain, the United Arab Emirates, and the Persian Gulf states. Although it took time to register and launch our products in each country, we were able to enter each market and find success fairly quickly. By 1983 Hikma had finally reached a break-even point. We were no longer running in the red.

Profits from our foreign sales increased, but shipping was costing us too much. A few years later, in the mid-1980s, the economy started tanking worldwide. The Syrian government suddenly wasn't able to pay us. Calling a debt collector wasn't a viable option, so I proposed something my father, my grandfather, and many others had used—a practice that had been around for thousands of years: bartering. Syria offered to pay me with a product I could turn around and sell in Jordan. After some debate we settled on peanuts.

That worked out for a while, but then the Syrian government started protecting their own pharmaceutical industry and told me they would no longer allow our products or any other Jordanian products to enter their country. That was fine with me. I didn't really want to keep working for peanuts anyway.

About that time I made the decision that Hikma should start backward integrating, meaning we would produce our own raw materials rather than buying them from others. Even though they were easy to obtain, I wanted to tighten the quality control on our medications and be independent of outside sources.

Finally, after a lot of time and red tape, the Saudi Arabian government allowed us to begin selling there. Hikma became the first company to sell generic drugs to the Saudis. That ended when the first Gulf War broke out a few years later. After Saddam Hussein and his Iraqi forces invaded Kuwait in 1990, the United States and the United Nations quickly formed a coalition of thirty-nine European and Middle Eastern nations, including Saudi Arabia, hoping to pressure Iraq into withdrawing. Jordan wished to remain neutral and refused to join the coalition, so Saudi Arabia and the smaller Gulf nations stopped accepting Jordanian products, including our Hikma medications.

Hikma had signed a contract with the Iraqi government prior to the war, so we continued to supply their doctors with medicine. We saved lives, but we lost many clients because of it.

The unstable Middle East is a difficult business environment. War has plagued me from childhood and uprooted my family several times. At times it cost us everything we owned. Now it was limiting my business. I knew it was time to expand my vision to the more stable, lucrative, and highly competitive regions of the United States and Europe—a plan that had always been my long-term goal.

Select Good Advisers

As the man walked around Hikma's Jordan facility, I kept trying to read his face, hoping to see a sign of encouragement.

We'd been up and running for only a few years, but I had big plans for the company. The United States was the top market, with Americans at that time (in 1982) consuming about 40 percent of all pharmaceuticals worldwide. (The United States remains the number-one market more than thirty years later followed by Japan, Germany, France, and China.)

I wanted to sell our Hikma generic drugs to that very large American market, but in order to achieve that we needed approval from the Food and Drug Administration (FDA), an agency of the US Department of Health and Human Services. No pharmaceutical manufacturer in the Middle East had ever achieved that. I was determined to be the first.

Not only do the pharmaceuticals manufactured for consumption in the United States have to be compliant with the FDA's current good manufacturing practice (cGMP) regulations, with each step documented, but the containers they're stored in have to meet specifications, as do the design, construction, and operation of the facilities where the drugs are manufactured.

I wanted to find a way to make sure each step of Hikma's manufacturing process and our plant were consistently up to the FDA's quality specifications. We were manufacturing generic drugs, and the FDA has special guidelines for that. We had to show the agency documented proof that our pharmaceuticals were meeting the same rigid standards as the innovator drugs we were copying, which meant our generics had to be manufactured with the same active ingredients as the original drugs (though the inactive drugs we were using could be different.) They had to be identical in quality, strength, dosage, and the way they were administered.

We were brand new and small, so I knew Hikma wasn't anywhere near being FDA compliant yet, but I had no doubt we could reach that level of quality. I just needed to know what changes I had to make and how I had to plan in order to reach that goal.

That's why I'd hired a consultant to tell us how Hikma could start preparing to gain FDA approval. The man, an Arab-American independent consultant who was originally from Jordan, checked out our factory, examined our paperwork, then turned to me and said, "You'll never be able to achieve FDA approval."

It was as if someone had punched me in the stomach. What kind of advice was that?

When I finally found my voice, I somehow managed to mutter a curt thank you then quickly ushered the man to the door. What a waste of money.

Despite his years in the United States receiving higher education, the man had maintained a limited, shortsighted Middle Eastern mind-set—something I'd failed to see before I'd hired him. I'd long ago embraced the Western mind-set and had far-sighted and far-reaching visions for Hikma, with FDA approval being a major goal I planned to use to set the course for our company in the coming years.

I'd selected the wrong adviser, but fortunately I made the right decision when I rejected his advice. Advisers can make or break a country, a company, or a relationship, and it's up to you to find the best ones you can. But just because someone appears qualified doesn't mean he or she is good for your company. What's good for one corporation may be detrimental to another.

You not only have to select the best advisers for your company and particular situation, but you also have to decide what action you're going to take based on what they recommend. As either the head of your company or a high-level corporate executive, you need to recognize whether advice is valuable and worth putting into action or dangerous to the future of your company. You have to decide whether you're going to act on it or reject it.

However, even brilliant people can get it wrong. Too often a good leader ignores great advice that would help his or her corporation and instead takes wrong advice that ultimately ends badly. Even after you carefully examine a person's credentials and his or her understanding of and fit with your company, ultimately you need to use your own knowledge and gut instincts to decide if that input is something you should risk. Too many people sell themselves short and go against their own years of stored-in-the-brain knowledge as they meekly agree to really horrible advice.

In addition to for-hire advisers, you need to evaluate carefully the advice coming from within your company—from your executives and board members. You may feel you trust them more because they know your business better than an outsider, but just because they work for you doesn't mean they always have the best advice.

On the other hand, they could be giving excellent guidance. There are times when even those who are a few steps down on the corporate ladder see a situation more clearly than you do because they're closer to the problems. In that case are you humble enough to take your employees' recommendations if they differ from your own?

The decision to take or reject advice lands with the boss. How effective are you at finding and taking the best advice?

Making Hikma FDA Compliant

After I showed the negative independent adviser to the door, I started looking for a new one. I still needed advice on how to make my manufacturing facility FDA compliant, but now I had a different list of qualifications for my new consultant, whoever he or she turned out to be. That person obviously needed to have the intelligence to give me good advice, but he or she also had to have an optimistic, go-for-it way of viewing things. That meant starting with the basic foundation that just about anything is possible if you are willing to work hard for it.

To me it also meant hiring someone with Western thinking who would help open American doors for me. So, in 1988, six years after that first negative adviser, I turned to the US Agency for International Development, which the late president John F. Kennedy had helped create in 1961 to provide economic, humanitarian, and developmental assistance to people overseas struggling to make better lives under difficult scenarios such as natural disasters or poverty. The agency also provided technical analysis, evaluation, and expertise for projects in developing or third-world countries that would benefit others while maintaining American values. My company definitely fit those guidelines.

USAID arranged for an expert consultant from the United States to come to Hikma, assess our company and our equipment, then give us a list of what we needed to do to become FDA approved. This adviser was excellent and gave us the necessary guidelines for improving our factory, especially our infrastructure such as our air-conditioning and dust-extraction systems. We needed to buy new machinery and make some structural changes to the plant—all things that would take a lot of money, but at least I now had a working blueprint and something for us all to aim toward to attain our goals.

We started implementing various parts of the adviser's list almost immediately. One of the first things we did was build a separate building for the manufacture of cephalosporins, a class of antibiotics. A year later we purchased Arab Medical Containers, a Jordanian company that manufactured plastics, because I wanted to switch from glass containers to plastic for our drugs as most American-owned pharmaceutical companies had. By owning the company, we could make sure the quality of the containers met FDA specifications. We had to make sure the plastic wouldn't leach into the medications stored in the containers or have any kind of chemical reaction.

I put Mazen in charge of that company. It took a while to correct a lot of the problems there, but by 1994 the plant was producing items to the specifications we needed. Not only that but Mazen was able to increase production from two million units a year to thirty million.

We were on our way to compliance.

As I went over the USAID adviser's list of what Hikma needed to add and change to become FDA approved, I suddenly realized it might be far easier to buy a manufacturing plant that was already FDA compliant. And what better place to do that than in the United States? Surely that would fast-track our approval.

Again I came in contact with a bad adviser. An international banker we approached told us we wouldn't succeed in the United States because we didn't have the products or experience to compete there. I chose to ignore his advice and instead went ahead with my vision, putting Said in charge of finding the perfect US facility Hikma could purchase for about US$2 million.

Two years later, after researching several companies, he found West-Ward Pharmaceutical Corporation, a facility in Eatontown, New Jersey, that manufactured generic drugs but was barely FDA compliant. The timing was a little awkward. Said first went to visit the plant right in the middle of the first Gulf War.

Iraq's former president, the late Saddam Hussein, had invaded Kuwait on August 2, 1990. Five days later the United States launched Operation Desert Shield. Saudi Arabia's rulers, fearing Iraq would invade them next, agreed to have US troops based out of their country. Five months later, on January 17, 1991, with Saddam Hussein still refusing to leave Kuwait, the United States began its air war against Iraq. A month later, on February 24, the United States and its coalition troops from around the world launched the ground war to free Kuwait.

In the middle of that war, Said and Ali Husry went to visit West-Ward for the first time. I'm sure a few people wondered why two men from the Middle East were trying to buy a pharmaceutical company less than an hour outside New York City. But by June of that year, we'd closed the deal for West-Ward, paying US$2.5 million cash for it. Unfortunately, West-Ward was in trouble on multiple fronts. The previous owners had let the quality slip, which meant we inherited their legal, FDA, and regulatory problems as well as the plant's antiquated technology. We brought in our own team from Hikma Jordan, who decided to hire new American managers and keep only a few of the original employees.

Over the next few years, we hired more outside advisers— four of the best American pharmaceutical consultants we could find—to help us turn around West-Ward and give further recommendations for our other facilities. A year before we'd purchased West-Ward, Hikma had started building a new facility in Portugal to service the European market better, particularly the areas the larger pharmaceutical companies were somewhat ignoring. All four advisers gave us excellent suggestions about all our plants, and we implemented what they recommended.

It took us three years, a lot of money, and new equipment to turn around the New Jersey facility. The FDA inspectors spent six months carefully examining the plant and our product line then, in 1994, agreed West-Ward was once again fully compliant. Even better, the FDA inspectors were so impressed with our American manufacturing facility and the way we conducted business, they started training their new employees at West-Ward to show them the quality they should be looking for in other plants. That was nice to hear, especially since the naysayer advisers over the years had tried to quash our dreams. As I'd predicted, our US plant led the way to our FDA compliance.

Meanwhile we'd been implementing the necessary changes at our Jordan plant too, but unlike our American plant, which needed only to regain its compliance, there we were starting from scratch. It took us a few years longer, but finally we were ready for our FDA inspections in Jordan. In May 1996 we hired a consultant to help us prepare the necessary paperwork. The FDA certified Hikma Jordan's manufacturing facility was acceptable, allowing us to start exporting one of our products—naproxen sodium, a non-steroidal, anti-inflammatory pain reliever—into the United States.

We became the first Arab company to become FDA acceptable. Five years later our new Hikma plant in Portugal also became FDA compliant.

I'm so glad I didn't listen to that adviser we hired in 1982.

Bad Business Advice

The corporate landscape is dotted with examples of bad advice. Take the example of New Coke, a marketing disaster still taught in business schools.

In the 1980s Coca-Cola hired market analysts whose research revealed older consumers were beginning to lean more toward diet drinks while younger ones wanted a sweeter taste than Coke offered. Sales figures at the time showed the company's main competitor, Pepsi, was beating out Coke at supermarkets, though Coke held the lead in restaurant and vending-machine sales.

Advisers recommended Coke come up with a new formula to beat the competition. Senior executives at Coke's headquarters in Atlanta, Georgia, including the vice president of marketing and the president of the US division, commissioned their chemists to come up with a new beverage. By 1985 the new drink was ready, and the marketing research team at Coca-Cola began blind taste testing it with small focus groups. The new soda got more favorable reviews than Coke or Pepsi, so the marketing staff advised the company to start producing it quickly, hoping to gain an advantage over Pepsi.

On April 23, 1985, the new-formula Coke was introduced to the world. Coca-Cola's then-chairman Roberto Goizueta announced the company would completely stop production of the old, familiar soda, and the company rolled out an ad campaign that said, "The best just got better."

What happened next wasn't what the advisers and marketing analysts had counted on: the consuming public revolted—loudly. Coca-Cola hadn't counted on loyal customers who had psychological attachments to the original taste. Consumers' letters and phone calls, in addition to public protests, were so opposed to the new drink that within three months, Coca-Cola made the decision to reintroduce the old formula, which the company branded "Classic Coke." Sales of the old formula soared, and eventually New Coke ceased production.

The advisers had looked at the sales figures, but they'd failed to realize how limited focus groups are and how loyal food consumers can be to a particular taste.

Some of the worst advice someone ever gave me was to go for the money and forget everything else—to hit and run, as I call it. They told me I should get as much as I could in as little time as possible and then run away once I'd made my quick gains. Horrible advice. Don't ever believe that's a way to build up a global corporation.

I most certainly have never wanted to give people inferior products, grab their money, and take off running. Instead my goal has always been not only to build a quality company with safe, reliable products but to be around for years to come, helping as many generations as possible.

Getting to Good Advice

When I first started Hikma, I listened carefully to an Italian friend of mine who was a marketing specialist at Eli Lilly. His advice was invaluable and helped me lay a solid foundation for my company.

In addition to that, I received sound wisdom from my family and closest friends: be persistent, and keep after your target until you succeed. That small group encouraged me over the years, and when things looked bleak I needed their encouragement. It kept me going. They kept reminding me that even when I faced difficulties, I needed to keep pushing forward, that I would succeed if I tried long and hard enough to accomplish my goals.

They were right.

That said, don't think friends and relatives are always the best choices to be your business advisers. You may know them, but do they really know what's necessary to solve your company's problems? You need seasoned professionals.

As they say, there's wisdom in a multitude of counselors. If possible try to form a group of wise people you trust, who know your business and industry well, then turn to them for advice. They won't always agree with each other, but ultimately they can help you make better decisions if you hear all their points of view. What's even better is if some of those advisers play devil's advocate and take opposite positions to make you justify your own. It makes you examine all points of an issue and reconsider things that might cause problems down the line. It also makes you realize whether you're asking the right questions.

That means you have to be willing to have someone disagree with you. If you're the type of leader who wants only yes-men around verifying every word you speak, you'll miss out on some good counsel.

What can be helpful is to get your group of advisers in the same room and have a brainstorming session, listening to each one as he or she not only makes his or her case but defends it against others' opposing points of view. That kind of setting, especially if it's in a casual and relaxed environment, can generate a healthy exchange of ideas—and a lot of possible solutions.

While you're at it, don't reject employees who aren't high-level executives. You'd be surprised what great ideas and solutions can come from those who are working in the trenches and haven't yet started their advances up the corporate ladder. They see things you don't, so give them credit for having creative thought processes too. After all, you thought enough of them to hire them; now listen to what they have to say.

Today Hikma still uses advisers. Some of our corporation's key consultants are from Merrill Lynch and Centerview, two of the leading investment-banking advisory and financial-management firms, both of which are based in New York. We also have an executive committee made up of Hikma's top management including my son, Said, who's been Hikma's chief executive since 2008.

As our company's nonexecutive chairman, I'm often called

upon to weigh in on different decisions at the company. After years of asking company executives and other experts for advice, I now find my years of experience have turned me into one of Hikma's expert advisers.

Well, I do know something about the company and the pharmaceutical industry.

Know How and When to Expand Manufacturing Internationally

I knew the next phase of Hikma's expansion had to be establishing a physical presence in Europe and the United States beyond exporting our products from our facility in Jordan. We needed to establish more manufacturing plants. I'd wanted to be concentrate on the Middle East, but wars and our clients' economic problems kept reducing our sales. If we didn't expand out of the region, we were never going to grow—and possibly wouldn't even survive. Hikma needed to gain access to the large American and European markets as quickly as possible.

We began our search in both regions simultaneously around 1989 and 1990.

My initial idea was to buy existing facilities and modify them to meet our needs. I figured we'd save time and, hopefully, money. Particularly in the United States, I wanted to find an existing pharmaceutical plant that was already FDA compliant.

As I mentioned I sent Said to the United States to find a pharmaceutical plant we could buy. He had the easier job. After all he was only dealing with one country. I had many nations in Europe to consider as I tried to decide where to base our operations.

I researched every country's size, location, market share, and workforce, ruling out anywhere the market was flooded with products from Big Pharma—the major pharmaceutical companies. We wouldn't be able to compete well in those markets.

Finally I narrowed my choices to Portugal, Greece, and Ireland. I was familiar with Portugal because I'd spent a lot of time there visiting a manufacturer that supplied raw materials to our factory in Amman. The more I visited the country, the more I liked it. For some reason it reminded me of Palestine, even down to having a long coastline along a major body of water just like the sea and beaches near my childhood home of Jaffa. It wasn't my familiar Mediterranean Sea, but I definitely didn't mind the Atlantic Ocean, especially after being somewhat landlocked in Jordan for so many years.

Being near water provided more benefits than just beauty—it also offered good culinary treasures. I was delighted to discover Portuguese restaurants always featured some of the best whitefish in the world, a favorite of mine.

Besides the abundance of natural beauty and great food, I found Portugal's people to be warm, open, and unspoiled. And there were twelve million of them, a large enough population to sustain our factory's operation and keep us afloat with domestic sales in case anything happened to delay exporting our products into other countries.

Portugal offered many positives. For one it was already part of the European Union, which meant Hikma would have access to a larger mainland market. And there was a great workforce we could tap. Five or six of the multinational drug companies had recently consolidated down to one or two plants in advance of the 1992 integration of the European Union, leaving many experienced pharmaceutical plant managers and workers unemployed. They were looking for jobs—and, hopefully, we would soon be able to provide them.

Locating a facility in an EU country had advantages, including size. The European Union provides a no-borders business market with access to five hundred million people, almost double America's three hundred million.

When I started expanding into Europe, the euro wasn't the common currency, but I knew many in the European Union had been pushing for it since the 1960s. That finally officially came to pass on January 1, 2002, when the euro replaced the currencies of twelve nations: Austria, Belgium, Finland, France, Germany, Greece, Ireland, Italy, Luxemburg, The Netherlands, Spain, and Portugal. Britain, Denmark, and Sweden retained their own currencies. Currently seventeen EU member states use the euro.

I finally decided Portugal was where we would establish our first foreign manufacturing plant and sent Ali Husry to find one we could buy. We determined our new Portuguese plant would produce injectables because there was a strong demand for them throughout Europe. We'd established a small formulation area for them at our Hikma Jordan facility in 1984, but we'd been able to produce only small quantities. Injectables are expensive to manufacture and require a very sterile environment in a factory that never shuts down. You have to be up and running 365 days a year in order to maintain the quality standards. To make any kind of profit, your plant has to fill at least 70 percent of its vials continuously during each manufacturing cycle. That means you have to produce a high volume and ship the drugs quickly if you're going to see any profits.

After a frustrating search, we slowly came to realize no existing facilities in Portugal met our specifications. I finally decided we needed to build one from scratch just as we'd done in Jordan. Ali began another search, this time to find land for us.

He soon located a great property in Sintra, about seventeen miles northwest of the capital, Lisbon, and ten miles from the ocean. It's a charming town located at the base of a mountain range, with a population of about thirty-three thousand. Sintra is popular with tourists because of its abundance of ancient estates, castles, and historic buildings, some dating back to the eighth and ninth centuries.

There was also the benefit of our property being located near a rail line and major highways into Lisbon and having access to an international airport—important considerations for shipping our products.

I wanted to oversee construction of our Portuguese facility as I had the one in Amman, so Samira and I found an apartment nearby. It was on the ninth floor, with a breathtaking view. We could even see the ocean if we stretched our necks and looked over the tops of some buildings.

Samira happily got busy buying furniture and decorating our new home—our sixteenth together counting all our moves through the Middle East, Italy, and the United States. She chose blue and gold as the main colors to symbolize the sea and sand and excitedly prepared the guest rooms for when our children and grandchildren would visit. Our whole family fell in love with Portugal.

Samira completed furnishing our apartment well before our contractors finished building our manufacturing plant. Just like when we had been building our facility in Amman, construction dragged on longer than I preferred, but our first build had shown me I needed to have patience. I found I wasn't as frustrated with the process the second time around. I'd already learned that when you build something of value that is meant to last, there are no shortcuts. Plus I had a lot of other Hikma business to keep me occupied.

I know there are always roadblocks of some kind in industry, and this time we were dealing with a foreign government, but I had faith we had a solid plan and everything would work out eventually. Hikma wasn't going to achieve global success overnight, but at least we'd have a factory built to the strictest standards of quality. I had to keep reminding myself of that to keep from panicking about how tight our money situation was. We were overextended, and, truth be told, building Hikma Portugal nearly bankrupted us. We'd just purchased West-Ward in New Jersey only to discover it needed millions in refurbishments to bring it back into FDA compliance. A lot of money was flying out the door. This definitely wasn't going as smoothly as I'd envisioned it in my head.

One thing that helped us during that difficult time was we'd established good relationships with our Portuguese builders and contractors, and they were patient whenever we had to delay payments to them. We felt terrible about it, but the entire time we were under construction, we were scrambling to try to get loans.

Jordanian banks weren't willing to loan us money, but the International Finance Corporation of the World Bank was because of a mandate at that time to help underdeveloped countries like Portugal. They gave us US$7 million—probably the only thing that saved us.

That's another good reason to expand into underdeveloped countries: there are organizations around the world willing to help financially. You just need to do your research to find them.

It took us three years to finish construction, but finally our state-of-the-art injectables facility, Hikma Farmaceutica, opened for business in 1993 complete with a talented sales force and an experienced local management team and workers. Originally the factory was divided into three main departments: ampule/vial liquid filling, cephalosporin powder filling, and a lyophilization freeze-drying department. Since then Hikma Portugal has undergone major expansions and modifications. In 2004 we built a new ampule department and two years later a new cephalosporin facility housing two modern, high-speed filling lines. A few years ago, we added a new lyophilization facility.

Today Hikma Farmaceutica's three hundred employees are split between three shifts producing seventy million units of thirty different injectable products, half of which get exported to our US clients, the rest evenly divided between our clients in Europe and the MENA region. We have enough demand for our products that for each run, we're at more than 75 percent of vial-filling capacity. I'm also pleased that about 70 percent of our Hikma Portugal staff is female.

Due to the extremely high regulatory standing the facility has with the FDA and European standards agencies, we're now developing and manufacturing pharmaceuticals for third-party clients and other drug companies. We export those to the United States, Europe, the Middle East, China, New Zealand, and Africa. We now ship more than US$30 million of injectables a year from our three Portuguese plants.

Establishing a Foreign Presence Beyond Exporting

Building a manufacturing facility in a foreign country is certainly a major decision for any corporation, requiring a lot of consideration and research. How do you know when to go from exporting your products from facilities in your home country to establishing a physical footprint in another country?

Probably the easiest answer is: when it makes more economic and business sense to do so. When you can serve your foreign customers better with a manufacturing or service facility closer to them, and you can afford to buy or construct facilities, do it. If your export point is thousands of miles away from a large base of your customers, and they are dissatisfied with the turnaround time, you need to start thinking about moving closer to them.

Will you save a substantial amount on shipping if you build a foreign facility? Will you be more competitive and able to add more clients? Are the country you're considering and its government politically stable? I'm used to instability. My world throughout my life has been unstable. I know how to navigate around that, but do you?

Will that foreign government try to insert itself into your company and become heavy handed in telling you how to do business? Is the currency stable? What's the inflation rate? What are your insurance costs going to be? What's the infrastructure like? Are there reliable utilities like water, electricity, phone, and the Internet?

Is the local population friendly to foreign-owned firms, or will it sabotage every move you make? Are you well versed in the country's language? Do you know the culture and understand the people? After all, they're going to be your employees.

If your management team is from your home country, will they be able to live safely abroad? What's the threat of terrorism there? Have you established a crisis management team to extract your employees quickly if need be?

Can you find land or an existing facility to buy near major transportation? Are you near a rail line, an airport, or major highways? You don't want to be in such an isolated area that it turns out shipping your supplies and products actually is faster from your home base.

Will you be able to get all the manufacturing materials you need easily? Will you be able to ship your products to customers in nearby foreign countries? What kind of relationship does the foreign country have with neighboring governments? What are the country's export and import laws in relation to where you want to ship your goods? What about tariff laws?

Today Hikma usually finds out about potential companies from our investment firm, which knows the specifications of the businesses we're interested in purchasing. Our team there sends us alerts whenever they find something that fits the description and location we give them, then we immediately check out the facilities to see if we're interested.

You may also hear about companies that are about to go on sale from those in your particular industry. And don't forget the daily, weekly, and biweekly magazines published exclusively for your industry. If you follow the news, you can generally find something to purchase.

The pharmaceutical industry is a small world, and everyone pretty much knows everyone else, so we frequently hear about opportunities by word of mouth. That's especially true in the Middle East, where there are maybe ten or fifteen top-tier pharmaceutical companies. At industry conferences we don't just talk about our products. We also discuss available companies.

But buying a multimillion-dollar company is always a bit tricky. The negotiation process can run anywhere from three months up to one or two years. The smart way to begin negotiations is to find out why the owners want to sell in the first place. Do some snooping. Is it a private, family owned, or publicly owned company? Are a good number of family members or shareholders interested in selling immediately? If so that gives you a good bargaining tool and usually speeds up the process quite a bit. On the other hand, if the owners are emotionally attached to their company, negotiations could drag on. Do you have the stamina to hang in there through all that? Only you know what your time restraints are.

These are all things you need to consider seriously before you buy or build in a foreign country.

Be Multifaceted and Cross-Train

As I looked over her resume, the young Jordanian woman sitting across from me tried to appear confident. Majda Labadi's educational credentials were impressive. I was pleased to see she'd obtained her bachelor's degree in business administration from the same school I'd attended—American University of Beirut. After graduating she'd returned to Jordan and worked for a few years before moving to Germany, where she'd earned her master's in health administration from Hochschule Für Okonomie (School of Economics) in Berlin.

As I chatted with her, I became even more impressed by her intelligence, drive, candor, and personality. She had wonderful potential. I had a feeling she'd be a great Hikma employee.

After returning from Germany, Majda had first looked for a job in hospital administration, but no hospitals in Jordan would hire her. She told me she thought they wanted to hire only male doctors for those positions.

(It's still debated worldwide whether physicians or those with backgrounds in business make better hospital administrators. Some say when doctors are running a hospital, the patient care is better. On the other hand, it doesn't do the patients much good if physician directors don't know much about business and cause the hospitals they're running to fail financially, particularly since the doctors have to answer to members of the hospitals' executive boards. If a facility can't buy necessary equipment or ends up shutting down completely, it's not serving anyone. Ideally the best administrator is a combination of both, but a person with that many skills can be difficult to find.)

I knew Majda would be a definite asset to our still-young company, but I didn't have an administration position available at that time. Instead, I told her, I wanted to hire her for a data-processing job in our computer department.

She was momentarily speechless then finally said, in all honesty, that she'd never even used a computer. That may sound odd today, but this was in May 1985. Not many people owned computers then. Personal computers as we know them were still in their infancy.

To put it into some perspective, consider that only ten years earlier, in 1975, IBM had produced the first "portable" computer, the IBM 5100—which weighed a dainty fifty-five pounds. That was the same year two young college dropouts named Bill Gates and Paul Allen established Microsoft. Steve Jobs and Steve Wozniak co-founded Apple Computer a year after that. Two years later, in June 1978, Apple introduced its first operating system, DOS 3.1, and three years after that IBM introduced a personal computer that ran the new MS-DOS operating system—the same year the Commodore VIC-20 became popular. Compaq Computer was founded the next year, in 1982.

When I interviewed Majda, the Apple Macintosh had been introduced only a year earlier, in 1984. So dealing with computers really was a strange, new territory for all of us. I told her a data-processing job in our computer department was the only position I had, and I was willing to take a chance on her if she were willing to take a chance on stepping out of her comfort zone to learn a new set of skills.

"If you're willing to teach me, I'm ready to learn," she said.

Majda did a great job learning about computers, which I think surprised her more than it did me. She did such a great job that six months later, we made her head of our purchasing department, which had about five employees at the time. Majda applied the computer skills she now had to her new position and began quickly improving the software and overall performance of the purchasing department.

Diversify and Cross-Train Your Employees

I've always believed in cross-training, or rotating people through different departments and international facilities. At Hikma we know there are many benefits to learning new skills as well as coming in contact with employees you've never worked with or even met.

I was never really a big proponent of specialization, probably because once I conquer a project or skill, I get a bit bored and start craving the challenge of something new. Eli Lilly taught me that the more functions you can perform, the better. My bosses moved me through different departments and jobs, which gave me chances to hone many of my skills—some I didn't even know I had until I was put in positions that required using them. But I soon realized the benefits, and when I started Hikma I knew to do the same thing with my employees. We still do that.

The more aspects of your company your employees know about, the more they make themselves invaluable to you. Hikma employees may not understand at first why we ask them to change departments, but they usually quickly discover it's not a demotion even if, in their perception, it's not an upward movement. Whether it's sideways or what appears to be "down two and over one," new job experiences are actually great training experiences.

When you add and reinforce many different skills, it's a lot like a gem cutter perfecting a diamond. The more facets are cut and polished on the stone, especially if they're done expertly, the more a diamond will sparkle. Many, many facets give a diamond its brilliance, and your employees' many skills do the same for your company. The only way to develop them is to keep employees in learning mode, moving them through positions as you add to their knowledge base.

Benefits of Cross-Training

There are many benefits to cross-training your employees. For one it keeps them from getting bored with doing the same thing every day (I definitely speak from experience on this). When you give them new challenges, they're less likely to suffer job burnout.

It also strengthens your team. If someone's working in only one office or part of your facility, he or she probably won't get opportunities to meet the majority of the other employees, particularly if your business is large or has international offices. Switching an employee's responsibilities gives him or her the opportunity to interact with new people he or she never realized were part of the same team. The more people each employee knows, the closer he or she feels to them, and the more unified your company becomes.

Not only that but people become more empathetic toward each other once they learn everything the other has to put up with on a given day. A salesman who's normally out among people and frequently traveling may never have realized how challenging it is for his fellow employees who spend their days staring at computer screens and never get out of their offices. By the same token, someone who rarely leaves the office may not realize how challenging it is to have to be energetically positive and uplifting the entire day while meeting with clients.

Cross-training also guarantees you'll always have someone who can confidently step into critical positions when the employees who usually handle those jobs are out sick or on vacations. That strengthens your company.

Not all employees will do well in new positions. Some people just don't like change and find comfort and even enjoyment in their daily routines. They do better with the known than the unknown. It's definitely challenging for some people when they're put into unfamiliar environments. It may take them a while to get comfortable with a new way of doing things and having different responsibilities.

But soon enough they and their bosses will discover their hidden skills—ones of which even they may not be aware. Your graphic designer may be incredibly artistic, but it's also possible he or she is gifted with numbers and is a wiz in the accounting department. You never know until you allow him or her to experience different settings and job responsibilities. Your warehouse manager may have a totally engaging personality and be a born salesman, but those skills aren't benefiting him or you in his current position, where he catalogs and shifts boxes of merchandise all day. The person in a detail-oriented job may actually turn out to be better at seeing the big picture and long-range planning. When you move people around, you find how much more they have to contribute to the company.

This brings a lot of personal satisfaction because when people are growing professionally and emotionally, they have more positive feelings of self-esteem.

Another benefit to cross-training is when you move people into different departments or positions, they bring new sets of eyes and ideas to the table. They may come up with unique and creative solutions to problems, suggesting ways to accomplish something that those who've been too close to the situation never considered. Those new ideas may end up not only being more efficient but also saving you money.

Cross-Training Leads to Promotions

Let's go back to Majda Labadi. After she worked for us a few years, I thought it might be good for her to gain the expertise only INSEAD could offer. Even though she already had a master's in administration, I knew INSEAD's intensive, three-week advanced-management program could teach her things she didn't know, and, though we didn't tell her at the time, we had much bigger plans for her.

Out of a class of twenty-nine students, she was the only one from the Middle East—and the only woman. It didn't bother her. Good thing because when she came back to Amman, we moved her into planning and operations by promoting her to plant manager at Hikma Jordan, a position where she once again had zero experience. Majda felt a little overwhelmed, but I let her know she could always come to me if she needed help.

That cross-training experience was a huge challenge for her. She had to organize the plant, manage the workers, develop training programs for them, and build unity and team spirit among them, all while dealing with compliance issues.

I know it can be quite a process educating some men about how capable women can be. We knew Majda's promotion would be not only an educational experience for her but a cross-training education for the employees who would be answering to her. Majda had done fine with her twenty-eight male classmates at INSEAD, but now she had to command the respect of two hundred employees, the majority of whom were male. On top of that, the previous manager had been an engineer, an older man many of the employees greatly respected.

During Majda's first week on the job, one of the male workers decided to challenge her authority in front of the others. The room got very quiet as Majda felt all eyes on her, everyone listening to see how she would handle the situation. She stood her ground, raised her voice to a commanding level, and told the man to get back to work, that he could talk to her privately in her office on his break if he had a problem. He backed down, and no one else challenged her after that.

Eventually the workers were able to see how much she cared about them, and they grew to trust her and the direction in which she was guiding the plant. They became as loyal to her as they had been to her male predecessor. Her leadership skills really had a chance to flourish in that position.

Majda brought new insights into many aspects of the job, particularly in her approach to filling large rush orders. She'd round up additional employees and managers from outside her department to lend helping hands then work through the evening until everything was processed, packed, and shipped.

That's what moving someone new into a position can do—bring new insights into how to solve problems.

Majda's always been very goal oriented and driven. She's a lot like me in constantly wanting to learn new skills and take on new adventures. Once she'd mastered the job of Hikma Jordan plant manager and director of operations, she asked the chairman of Hikma, who by that time was my son, Said, to give her another challenge. He made her strategy manager of a new department we'd just created: business development at Hikma Investments. She excelled at that. She conquered each new venture we gave her and brought in winning results even when she had what appeared to be less experience than the job would require.

Around the world the conventional wisdom when a company has an employment opening is either to advance the next person in line in that department or to hire someone from outside with similar qualifications as the one who'd previously held the position. Sometimes that is the best solution, but not always. I'm a firm believer that many times you can bring in someone from another department with what appears to be completely different skill sets and achieve much-more-successful results. That's because it's the people who make the difference. Accumulated skills from what appear to be different or even opposing job positions sometimes will create a better job environment for those working in that department, plus bring new vision to solve old, unresolved problems.

When Hikma was first starting, we hired everyone from outside. We had to. But as we grew internationally, we recognized that our loyal employees, even if we moved them into new, unfamiliar jobs, would sometimes give us better results than unknown people. Plus this practice aided us in grooming our existing employees for the top positions in our corporation.

That's not to say we don't hire from outside. We have to because we're growing and expanding around the world, adding to existing facilities, and buying new companies. And, of course, people retire or move on to other ventures. But we like to discover as many of an employee's skill sets and talents as possible. The only way to do that is to put him or her in different positions and scenarios to see how he or she reacts and if he or she can perform successfully. How well does this person operate under pressure? Does he or she crack and start screaming at others, or does he or she rise to the occasion and come up with creative problem solving?

In 2001, after Hikma Farmaceutica had received FDA acceptance in America and approval from the Medicines and Healthcare Products Regulatory Agency (MHRA) in the United Kingdon, thus gaining the ability to sell our pharmaceuticals in both the United States and Britain, Said asked Majda to take over as general manager in Portugal. Once again she was asked to step into a completely new experience.

Majda was from Jordan, and though she'd attended universities in Lebanon and Germany then completed postgraduate work in France, she hadn't lived abroad in many years. Now we were asking her to move 2,500 miles away from her family and friends in order to supervise one of our plants staffed mainly with Portuguese employees. It wasn't going to be easy, but Majda readily agreed to the challenge.

Once again she brought fresh ideas to a new position and immediately began addressing the problem of high personnel turnover there. Soon after we'd completed our facility in Portugal, we'd hired mainly local people to staff it, including our managers—something we usually do with our manufacturing plants. We felt we'd hired well, and they were good employees, but for some reason the facility wasn't producing.

To try to figure out what was wrong, Majda and some of our experienced management staff from Hikma Jordan observed the employees for more than two months. She and our executive team didn't speak much Portuguese, but through translators and observation they soon discovered what some of the problems were.

Many of the employees we'd hired had formerly worked for other multinational pharmaceutical plants in Portugal but had lost their jobs when those drug companies had consolidated. That worked out well for Hikma because we needed to hire for our new manufacturing plant near Lisbon. The good thing was we weren't starting from scratch since our Portuguese employees were used to working at pharmaceutical plants.

The problem was most of them had been practically glued to their desks at their former jobs, isolated from their coworkers as they had each specialized in only one department. They lacked incentive because many of them had never been challenged to grow.

Their former employers hadn't encouraged too much team spirit or unity either, and our newly hired workers brought that with them—something they had to unlearn at Hikma. Their former employers had never encouraged them to consider how they fit into those companies' global enterprises. The result was they'd spent years never feeling as if they were part of anything larger than themselves.

Worse than that the positions they were in at Hikma didn't always match their abilities. Their work was similar to what they'd done in their previous jobs, but that didn't mean they'd been successfully placed then either.

Majda used the same cross-training she'd experienced at Hikma Jordan. She took the time to talk to and get to know all employees individually and carefully observed them for their strengths and weaknesses, then she and her team moved them into different positions she thought would better fit their talents. Majda didn't lay off a single worker. She and her team merely uncovered what employees were capable of and placed them in positions that were better suited to their particular skills.

That may sound simple, but it's not always easy getting people into jobs where they can produce the most.

The result was many of the employees began to enjoy their work more. They were finally in positions where their true skills and interests were being utilized; they were not just doing the same old things they'd been trained to do for years in their previous jobs.

But that wasn't the total solution. The more Majda talked to workers and managers and watched the production line of injectable powdered cephalosporins (antibiotics), the more she became convinced the employees didn't have the same Team Hikma vision as those in Jordan. She realized the management team and workers from Portugal weren't looking at long-term objectives or understanding where each part of the operation fit into the entire process.

To remedy that and help them see how they were parts of a team, she sent many to Amman so they could discover for themselves how they were part of the Hikma family and culture. She introduced employee bonuses and company cars, encouraged some to further their educations, and sent others into shorter, more-intense training courses.

Since Christmas is such a huge and elaborate holiday in Portugal, Majda had the management team enact a yearly tradition of throwing a corporate Christmas party to reward employees for achieving their yearlong targets. Managers told workers the more they exceeded the plant's annual objectives, the more elaborate their party would be—a definite incentive for the fun-loving employees.

At the Christmas party, before employees could begin knocking back the champagne, Majda told everyone how well they'd done and how much they were to be congratulated—then told them what the objective was going to be for the next year. They now had a new goal to work toward.

Needless to say, the employees' morale and job performances quickly improved. So did the facility's financials. Hikma Farmaceutica had been experiencing a cash-flow problem prior to Majda's taking over, but under her very capable leadership, sales increased 23 percent.

Two years after she started managing Hikma Portugal, we added a new warehouse and expanded our production lines, which more than tripled the liquid-injectables department for a combined annual output of more than seventy million vials of medication.

Our corporate philosophy at Hikma has always been that if a company invests in its employees, the employees become committed to the company. That's exactly what happened at Hikma Farmaceutica. Majda rose to become vice president of all our global injectables then, in February 2009, became corporate vice president of Hikma's human resources. She's also working on her doctorate in business administration from Instituto de Empresa in Madrid, Spain.

All the experience she's gained in purchasing, operations, business development, and general management she's given back to Hikma many times over, helping us to grow as she's grown her new skills, all while earning the respect of operational and corporate employees.

Square Pegs Don't Fit into Round Holes

Sometimes you need to shift workers to find positions that best utilize their talents. Many times, either because of family pressure or selecting wrong professions when first starting out in their careers, people come to you with résumés that are all wrong for their real skills. It's possible they may be excellent at jobs they never considered doing and where they have no experience. They're square pegs residing very uncomfortably in round holes, probably wobbling a lot because they're not fully secured in those wrong positions.

That's not to say they're not very good, hardworking employees and valuable people who are loyal to you and your company. You don't want to lose them, but you may need to shift them. It may be up to you and your human-resources department to find the right slots for them. An employee may be enthusiastic and have the desire to do any task you assign to him or her, but sometimes you have to face the fact that he or she may not be capable of accomplishing it.

What I've found over the years is you can use a mallet to flail away all you want on a square wooden peg, but all your pounding isn't going to make it fit into that round hole. If it's not a fit, it's not a fit.

Instead you really have to get to know your employees to figure out where their skills and interests lie. Take the time to observe them in all kinds of situations. Some things you just can't master no matter how much you try. But even if their natural abilities don't seem at first glance to be in areas where they have interests, it's possible the skill sets are hidden, or their strong desire will make up for any gaps. Some things you can learn even if you don't have a strong natural ability for them.

Cross-training your employees to expand their talents and skills benefits them and your company.

Samih and Samira's wedding.

Samih's graduation from AUB, 1954.

Physicians visiting Hikma's quality-control laboratories, headed by the minister of health.

Visit from Bahrain's minister of energy, 1985.

Visit from the minister of health and mayor of Wadi El Seer, 1980.

Samih and Samira in Japan.

Samih and Samira in China.

Inauguration of the Samih Darwazah Center for Innovation Management and Entrepreneurship, AUB.

Said speaking at the inauguration of the Samih Darwazah Center.

The family at the inauguration of the Samih Darwazah Center.

Samih with President Peter Dorman of AUB at the inauguration of the Samih Darwazah Center.

The inauguration of the cephalosporins plant in Portugal.

His Majesty King Abdullah II of Jordan at the inauguration of the cephalosporins plant in Portugal.

Samih receiving an honorary doctorate from St. Louis College of Pharmacy, May 2010.

World Entrepreneur of the Year 2008, Monaco.

World Entrepreneur of the Year 2008, Monaco.

The family, 1992.

Shobak school.

Friends and family gathered to celebrate Samih's retirement on May 14, 2014, in London, England.

Samira and Hana.

Samih thanking all those who helped make the night one to remember.

Samih with the Hikma board.

Samira and Samih.

Truly enjoying the evening.

Samira laughs with family friend Larry Leichman.

Trading stories with friends.

LESSON ELEVEN

Realize Problems Are
Good Reasons to Upgrade

Our second expansion overseas was going on simultaneously with our building of Hikma Portugal. Establishing a facility in the United States and selling to that large market had been my goal from the very beginning.

When my son, Said, discovered West-Ward Pharmaceuticals in Eatontown, New Jersey, in 1991, we knew that would be a great first entry into America. About US$2.5 million later, it was ours. Yes, it had been FDA compliant when we'd bought it, but the facility was old, with equipment that needed to be replaced. We knew there were problems. We spent the next few years and millions of dollars completely refurbishing it and restaffing to regain that FDA acceptance. But it was worth it.

West-Ward, under Said's capable management, experienced rapid growth as we'd hoped it would. We hit the break-even point by 1996 then expanded, building a second facility in the late 1990s and a third in 2003.

But equipment ages, and in an industry as precise as pharmaceuticals, you have to be installing new technology constantly. When we started having problems and computer glitches with the machines, we knew it might be an indication of more-serious problems that might lead to millions in upgrades.

We were right.

The February 3, 2012, letter from the FDA didn't tell us anything we didn't already know: West-Ward had problems.

Be Detail Oriented

I'm a stickler for details. In my industry I have to be.

At Hikma we keep very detailed records of our production processes and each activity performed in our manufacturing facilities. The very few times we've found Hikma employees altering information in some way or compromising our products' quality, we've fired them immediately.

Our machines are now all computerized, which makes quality control easier. We store our records not only in our computers but also as hard copies for when FDA inspectors visit our plants. Most inspections last a week.

Unfortunately computers can fail or have problems, and machinery can break down and begin acting erratically. Which is what happened at West-Ward.

It's good if you can have a system of fact checking at each of your facilities, with more than one person responsible for each area. There should always be at least two sets of eyes making sure no problems occur. Your managers and CEOs need to be aboveboard with every issue, honestly reporting problems and not covering up any mistakes.

I first learned about Alexander Graham Bell when I was working on my master's degree at St. Louis College of Pharmacy. Bell, a Scotsman who had immigrated to the United States, was an audiologist who invented the telephone and cofounded the Bell Telephone Company. What many may not realize is Bell also started the system of statistical quality control in industry. His system carried over to the pharmaceutical industry, where a group of scientists established "pharmacopoeia" quality standards listing all the preparations for producing medications and the uniform standards they should meet.

When I first started Hikma, I established our foundation for quality medications: we begin with the standards of the pharmacopoeia then impose even stricter standards.

I've seen what happens when governments of countries try to skimp on quality. When I was working for Eli Lilly and traveled to Iran, I noticed independent pharmaceutical companies there didn't want much oversight or input from Big Pharma. They were doing their own things. One company that manufactured contraceptive pills apparently hadn't done their research. They didn't realize the female hormone progesterone, used in making the pills, could permeate the skin, and they hadn't taken any precautions to protect their workers. The result was the men working on the assembly line were exposed to high levels of the hormone, and their breasts started to grow.

Details matter.

Our Entry into the US Market

The Greene brothers had first established the small, family-owned West-Ward Pharmaceutical Corporation in the 1940s. The two were chemists; they maintained high production standards in their facility and, up until the late 1980s, supplied their drugs to several large hospital chains. But in 1988 a large drug wholesaler bought the manufacturing arm of the company, and those standards dropped dramatically.

By the time Said discovered the company in 1991, the FDA was challenging West-Ward's quality control. We knew that when we bought the company, but we were confident our technicians and engineers could bring the facility's production values back up to meet FDA regulations within a few years.

We paid for the company in cash and, since banks wouldn't support us in the venture, found help instead from the Council of Development in New Jersey, which guaranteed bonds for us to issue. The local banks bought the bonds immediately, and that gave us the capital we needed for the refurbishment.

Good thing because we needed every penny of that investment. West-Ward was in bad shape with legal trouble, FDA issues, and regulatory problems. Said; his wife, Mami; and his two sons moved to New Jersey so he could oversee West-Ward's turnaround, and we hired a few new managers including a quality-control expert. Hikma also brought over our own team of managers and technicians from Jordan because we couldn't afford to put a second team in place in New Jersey. We retained as many of West-Ward's former staff as we could but immediately began retraining them in order to meet government guidelines for FDA approval.

West-Ward's first five years in the United States were difficult. We spent a lot of time, money, resources, and energy rebuilding the plant. Plus, customers started returning many of the products the previous owners had sold when they reached their expiration dates. We bit the bullet and took back all the products in order to maintain good relations with our clients.

We started with less than US$3 million in sales our first year, but a little more than a decade later the company had a turnover of about US$100 million annually and employed more than two hundred workers.

Today West-Ward develops, manufactures, and markets a broad range of prescription and over-the-counter medicines for pain relief, epilepsy, high blood pressure, heart problems, psychological disorders, and asthma as well as controlled-release and sustained-release products and sterile, high-potency pharmaceuticals. Not only that but we're constantly formulating new products in our research and development department. We serve more than 150 industry clients with all types of products and in all markets, including many of the world's leading pharmaceutical companies.

Why It's Better to Have More Than One Facility Doing the Same Thing

Running into problems with one of your manufacturing plants is a good reason to make sure you have other facilities and resources that can continue to supply your products to your customers. Always have a backup plan. Fortunately the problems that came with West-Ward's manufacturing plant didn't affect Hikma's overall bottom line too much.

In February 2012 the FDA sent us a warning letter about problems we were experiencing in our tablet-making facility at our Eatontown plant. Something had gone wrong with our production line, causing our generic lithium tablets not to meet size specifications. The FDA also told us our lithium carbonate tablets, the slow-release version bipolar patients usually take, weren't achieving the proper dissolution rate.

We were also having problems with our generic digoxin tablets not meeting size specifications. Doxycycline is used to treat some sexually transmitted diseases and even people who have been exposed to anthrax, but its main purpose is treating Lyme disease.

For months we kept changing our manufacturing process, trying to fix the problem, but the equipment just wasn't allowing the production line to operate the way we needed. The only option we had left was drastic, but it needed to be done.

After months of tweaking and adjusting, in November we took the entire line off production to fix the problem. We knew it would probably take a couple months, but we simply couldn't put up with the products not being totally perfect. Upgrading the equipment and making all the necessary changes ran us about US$30 million. That's a lot, but when you consider how much upgrades pay for themselves throughout the years and Hikma's basic principle not to settle for low quality in anything, it was just a necessary expense we had to absorb.

We restarted the line a month later but not at full capacity, so we could make sure everything was OK. The downtime caused us to lose a third of our sales—a US$21 million loss. Fortunately we also manufacture generic doxycycline at our FDA-compliant facility in Jordan, so we were able to keep supplying our customers. We were even able to obtain a higher price for the drug because other manufacturers were having production problems and making smaller amounts. The ancient economic principle of supply and demand applies to pharmaceuticals just as it does to any other manufactured item or even harvested crop such as wheat. If there's a shortage of a product, you can sell it for more because demand exceeds supply. Conversely, if you and your competitors are flooding the marketplace with an abundance of your product, you won't be able to charge as much because supply exceeds demand.

Fortunately upgrades to our equipment soon got our production line at West-Ward back on track and running well.

Keep Expanding

We've always been interested in expanding in the United States, and in October 2010 we bought Baxter Healthcare's Multi-Source Injectables's generics business in Cherry Hill, New Jersey, about seventy miles from our West-Ward facility. The US$112 million acquisition doubled the size of our global injectables business and doubled our sales in the US market, making us America's second-largest generic injectables supplier by volume. Our yearly sales from the plant now top US$470 million, so we've more than made up the purchase price.

The Baxter acquisition gave Hikma a 372,000-square-foot state-of-the-art manufacturing facility for the high-speed filling of vials plus a 100,000-square-foot warehouse and distribution center near Memphis, Tennessee.

Keep Looking for Opportunities to Expand Internationally

A fter all the heated emotions died down following the end of the first Gulf War in 1991, Saudi Arabia once again opened its borders to trade, and we decided to try to get our Hikma products back into the country.

Wars in the region had dealt us many economic blows, but we felt it was important to keep a strong presence in the MENA region, especially in Saudi Arabia. After all Hikma was an Arab company first and foremost, and we had a deep sense of civic duty to the people in the area. They were our original customers and, more importantly, our countrymen and neighbors. At its core Hikma would always be their local company no matter how big we grew.

But this time we decided to establish a physical presence there instead of shipping exports from Hikma Jordan. Foreigners were allowed to hold at most 49 percent ownership of a company, but we came up with a way around the minority share. We found two Saudi partners who were willing to join us to build Jazeera Pharmaceutical Industries. They owned 51 percent of the company split equally between them, and we held 49 percent, so of the three parties we actually did hold a majority share.

We chose Saudi Arabia's capital city, Riyahd, as the location to build our US$35 million factory and found a suitable piece of land in an industrial area. We had engineers from Hikma Jordan move there to oversee construction, so it would be to our specifications. That's definitely something to consider when building overseas. How quality minded is the local building industry? Do most engineers and construction workers come from that country, or are they immigrants from a third country?

Some estimates say at least 90 percent of the unskilled labor force in Saudi Arabia, including the building industry, is made up of foreign workers, particularly from the Philippines. That's because since the 1970s oil boom, most Saudi nationals have found it more lucrative to work in white-collar jobs. Not many are willing to earn the low wages associated with construction or other unskilled labor.

We decided having our own engineers supervise the construction was the best way to guarantee quality. The plant was completed in 1999, and after four years JPI started making a profit. By then the Saudi government had agreed to allow foreigners to own 100-percent shares of businesses, so I decided to offer our partners buyouts.

Before I brought up the subject with them, I told Khader Jarwan, Hikma's general manager in Jordan, to work with the international financial and consulting firm Ernst & Young to come up with an honest evaluation of our company's worth. I wanted to make sure we offered our partners a fair prices. My father always taught me if you take on partners, you have to take care of them. You always put their needs before your own.

I also told Khader to look at JPI and be objective about its potential, its future profitability, and any liabilities. He did exactly that, even projecting the value as 10 percent higher than what Ernst & Young had figured. That was fine with me. I wanted to give our partners exactly what they deserved, especially since without their support we wouldn't have been able to do business in Saudi Arabia. I was especially thrilled to hear Khader was so optimistic about JPI's future earnings.

Our Saudi partners were pleased with our offer and took their buyouts in 2006, the same year we received FDA approval for the facility. We became one of the first foreign-owned companies in Saudi Arabia.

Khader stayed at the facility and not only implemented all the standard Hikma policies and procedures but also skillfully merged our sales team from Hikma Jordan with the one at Jazeera. It took about a year to make the full transition. We had about a 50-percent loss in sales during that time, but we were more concerned with restructuring the company to fit our corporate culture. We respected the local Saudi culture, but we needed to make this company 100-percent Hikma.

Two years later Khader's forecast about Jazeera Pharmaceuticals's profitability materialized. We'd also gained a strong reputation in the local community for quality, transparency, honesty, and caring. It was Hikma through and through.

A few years later, Saudi Arabia's political relations with Jordan once again became strained, and the door slammed shut on all Jordanian imports. That meant we couldn't bring in any products from Hikma Jordan in Amman for JPI to distribute. The ban forced some Jordanian companies in Saudi Arabia to shut their offices and lay off all their employees.

We refused to close down and kept paying all our workers at Jazeera Pharmaceuticals, even when we didn't have anything to sell.

When one Saudi medical rep from JPI came to visit Hikma Jordan, he asked me, "When are you going to fire us? There's no business there."

"We're in this as a team," I said. "We either live together or die together. As long as Hikma is surviving, so will you."

What's true of partners is also true of employees and customers: you always take care of the people who have helped take care of you.

The situation eventually turned around, and in 2009 the FDA approved our manufacturing facility in Riyadh for the production of oral cephalosporins. That year we more than doubled our exports from Saudi Arabia to the United States.

Expanding into Europe, Asia, and Africa

In May 2000 Hikma reached another major milestone when our Jordan facility received approval from the Medical Control Agency (now the Medicines and Health Care Regulatory Agency) to register and sell its products in Great Britain and the wider

European Union. The MHCRA is the United Kingdom's equivalent of America's FDA, giving us access to more markets and showing how high our quality standards are.

Coming Home to Italy

With acquisitions in America and the Middle East, I felt it was time to concentrate on Hikma's further expansion into Europe—and what better place than Italy, my former home?

The European Union's still divided by different cultures, languages, and traditions, but on the whole, EU countries tend to support one another and encourage a uniform standard of quality.

Another key advantage of expanding into Europe was the relatively high standard of living. Why be in business if you can't sell your products and make a profit?

Of course, because I'd lived and worked in Rome for many years when I was with Eli Lilly, Italy held a special place in my heart. I knew the country, the language, the warmly generous people, and their beautifully artistic culture. Now I was going back as the owner of my own company. I couldn't wait to set up a Hikma facility there.

When I first started looking for a company to buy, I tried to find a local lawyer to help us, but attorneys' rates were far more than we were willing to pay. So instead I brought in Hikma's financial experts to help us.

Between us we managed to find a good prospect: Instituto Biochimico Pavese Pharma, a company in northern Italy that specialized in freeze-drying blood, plasma, and other biological substances. IBP, located in the ancient town of Pavia, about twenty-two miles south of Milan, was near the borders of France, Switzerland, and Liechtenstein. The company had one building, a small piece of farmland, and a whole lot of debt associated with the property, but once we started negotiations with the banks we were able to obtain better rates.

IBP officially became Hikma Italia in 2005. We'd initially planned to expand the building onto the farmland, which was included in the purchase price, but quickly discovered we couldn't. The Italian government said it had to remain agricultural land and couldn't be developed for industry—even though the previous owner had built an industrial facility right next to it.

It didn't make sense to us, but, like I've said, always have a plan B. Things will never go exactly as you think (or hope) they will.

Fortunately the facility had most of what we needed, so we made minor adjustments, which improved the overall layout, then added a cafeteria for employees. The zoning laws haven't changed. The government still won't let us develop the farmland. But that did get me thinking about what we could do with it besides park cows on it. Italy's famous for its many varieties of wines, and red wines do happen to have medicinal value. Maybe we could plant a nice vineyard there and start Hikma Winery.

Moving into Germany with the Art of Negotiation

Hikma had long considered moving into Germany for a number of reasons. Besides the country's being a power hitter in the European Union and being strategically located in the heart of Europe, its citizens are extremely quality oriented. German technology is first rate. Their standards match Hikma's.

In 2007 I discovered Thymoorgan, a small, privately owned company established in 1980—around the same time I'd started Hikma. It was located in the picturesque, mainly agricultural village of Vienenburg in Lower Saxony, about sixty miles southeast of Hanover.

Thymoorgan's founder and owner was a physician who'd created an extract of the thymus gland, a formulation some believed helped with physical rejuvenation. The Swedes in particular had embraced it enthusiastically and made up his largest market.

The doctor had made a fortune from sales of his product when he'd first started, but the extracts were expensive, and the public eventually lost interest. He was passionate about his product, but unfortunately not too many others were.

To stay afloat he'd shifted to marketing products used in the treatment of cancer, but those weren't doing well either. He knew he had no choice but to sell his company. I met with the doctor a number of times over the course of six months to discuss the terms of an acquisition. Since I saw the potential value of his company and the passion he had for what he'd built, I agreed to his initial price.

Because I'd so readily said yes, he started thinking maybe he could get more. The next time we met, he told me he now wanted more money for the business. As soon as I heard that, I closed my briefcase and got up to leave.

When you reach an agreement, you complete the transaction. If one party tries to break that agreement, you move on and find something else. Don't ever become so emotionally attached to a business that you're held hostage during negotiations. You know what you can afford to pay. If the owner won't agree to that price, calmly and coolly walk away. There are other businesses and other properties out there.

If there's one thing my family and the merchants in the Middle East have taught me, it's how to barter, haggle, and never back down from a price. We love a bargain, but we're fair—and tough. You'd better bring your A game to the table when you negotiate with us.

I went on my way and mentally dismissed Thymoorgan as I continued to search for a German company Hikma could buy. But about a month after our meeting, the doctor contacted me again and asked me to come back to Germany. When I walked into the meeting, there sat his accountants, I suppose in an effort to intimidate me with their expertise. They all told me I'd have to pay more if I wanted the business because the owner wasn't willing to accept the initial price we'd agreed upon, and they'd advised him he was correct.

They had called me back to Germany for that?

"I'm not changing my offer," I flatly told the doctor, looking him straight in the eyes. "Your accountants are trying to make more money for themselves from this deal, but that hasn't persuaded me in the least. My first offer is my final offer. Take it or leave it."

He looked at his accountants, and I got up to leave, irritated I'd wasted precious time on an international trip that had been a repeat of the previous meeting. I was determined not to put any more time into this venture.

The owner panicked and changed his tune, hastily deciding to override his and his accountants' greed. He took my offer and sold his business. We closed the deal in April 2007, and Hikma Thymoorgan was born.

We decided to add more manufacturing to the facility and develop new oncology products to sell to nearby countries and export to the United States. We also added innovative pharmaceutical technology. Three years later the plant received FDA approval.

Because I had kept looking around, I'd found another Germany facility that interested me. That's what I mean about not getting too emotionally involved in a sale: if you do, you may miss out on other wonderful opportunities.

A few months before Hikma bought Thymoorgan, we had purchased Ribosepharm, a privately owned company in Gräfelfing, Germany, just west of Munich. Ribosepharm specialized in the manufacture of injectable cancer medicines, including those used in the treatment of colorectal tumors and hematologic diseases.

Why settle for one German company when you can have two?

To handle the legal matters associated with both acquisitions, Hikma hired Ashurst, a law firm with offices in cities around the world, including London, New York, and throughout the MENA region. Always make sure you have good attorneys whether you're expanding locally or overseas.

A few years later, in 2010, we expanded our influence in Europe when we entered into a partnership with the Swiss firm Vifor Pharma. Hikma and Vifor now market and distribute to the MENA region an innovative treatment for iron deficiency.

Patience, Persistence, and Growth in Egypt

As I mentioned in the first chapter, for years Hikma had tried to enter the Egyptian market through the normal procedures of registering products there, but exporting those products from Amman was always difficult due to political considerations. In fact it reached a point where the Egyptian government refused to allow any imports from Jordan.

It seemed as if the only way we could get our products into the country was to manufacture there, so we started looking for an opportunity to merge with an Egyptian company.

Initially I met with the CEOs of two major corporations. Both seemed interested, but when I returned for a second meeting with the one in Cairo a few days later, he'd changed his mind.

"My financial people say you're like a whale," he said. "You'll swallow us whole."

I didn't know whether to be insulted that he was calling me a whale or flattered that Hikma was now regarded as such a strong presence in the pharmaceutical industry.

"We're not a whale, and we're not here to eat anybody," I calmly replied. "We want a merger, not a buyout."

He wasn't convinced and showed me the door.

We changed tactics and started looking for a smaller company that would allow us to get a foothold in Egypt. My son, Mazen, finally closed the deal with a private company called Alkan Pharma, which manufactured 175 solid and liquid generic drugs. It was Mazen's first major role in acquisitions, and it was impressive because we'd been trying—and failing—to get into Egypt for fifteen years. In August 2007 we purchased Alkan Pharma for US$60.5 million, and it became Hikma Egypt.

After the acquisition one of the first things I did was request Hikma's board of directors hold their annual meeting in Cairo and combine it with a ceremony for the opening of our new company. Dr. Hatem El-Gabaly, Egypt's minister of health, and Rasheed Mohamed Rasheed, the minister of foreign trade and industry, both joined us for lunch in the plant's cafeteria.

In the years since we purchased Alkan Pharma, Hikma Egypt has more than doubled its production.

Years ago we made a commitment to help Egypt even when the government made it difficult for us to do so. But we're dedicated to the health of the country's more than eighty-two million citizens, especially in these challenging times. In spite of the civil unrest and political upheaval in Egypt, we've recently invested even more there. In January 2013 we expanded by buying a second company, the Egyptian Company for Pharmaceuticals and Chemical Industries (EPCI). The US$22.2 million purchase of EPCI from a consortium of its shareholders brought thirty-five more products into our portfolio and gave us additional manufacturing capabilities, including a dedicated cephalosporin facility. Some of the pharmaceuticals produced there have also given us an entry into eye care and the growing ophthalmology market.

Buying Back a Former Darwazah Company to Gain Algeria

In 2007 Hikma was given an opportunity to buy back what I'd once owned. In 1962 I'd helped found Arab Pharmaceutical Manufacturing (APM) in Amman, the first drug-manufacturing facility in Jordan. I was also a member of the company's board of directors before I'd moved to the United States to get my master's at St. Louis School of Pharmacy.

After I left the company, APM continued to grow and began exporting to Arab countries, but its main source of income was its contracts with Jordan's Ministry of Health and armed forces. Then the Jordanian government changed course and moved on to other vendors. The loss of those contracts hit APM hard— one reason you should never limit the bulk of your company's financial health and clientele to only one or two large customers. Sales slowed so much, the company was on the verge of closing its doors. The only option that made sense was to try to get some money out of it by selling it.

When Said, who had just resumed his position as CEO of Hikma after serving in a Jordanian government position, discovered APM was for sale, he saw some value in it for our company. True, there was a sentimental factor in buying back something I'd helped start, but APM also gave us access to their production line of oral, injectable, and dermatological products, including an antiviral product the FDA had recently given approval to manufacture for distribution in the United States.

But it was APM's expansion into a North African country that was the most appealing to Hikma. APM provided opportunities for us that we'd been unable to achieve in Algeria.

After I'd left APM, the remaining owners had purchased a 50-percent stake in Al Dar Al Arabia, a manufacturing facility in Algeria that specialized in producing penicillin. APM had helped build the plant in 2005 along with their Algerian partner, Dar Al Dawa Development & Investment Company.

Hikma had first entered the Algerian market in the early 1990s, but at that time the country had a lot of political trouble along with six years of civil war that left more than one hundred thousand dead. It was also dealing with terrorism against foreign workers, which resulted in frequent kidnappings and assassinations.

That instability actually gave us a bit of an advantage because many international companies were too afraid to set up business in Algeria. Being from the Middle East, we were familiar with chaos and war. We decided Hikma could work there and still keep our people safe.

However, we couldn't circumnavigate Algeria's protectionism laws, which banned some pharmaceutical imports, including many of ours. The bottom line was we couldn't sell many products. One good thing was Mazen and other Hikma employees helped established pharmaceutical standards in the country, which helped safeguard the people.

Then came the opportunity for Hikma to buy Arab Pharmaceutical Manufacturing. We paid US$163.6 million, giving us that 50-percent stake of the manufacturing facility in Algeria. We were finally able to make some headway in that country—something that had eluded Hikma for years. We did have to invest some money to bring the plant up to our standards, but it was worth it.

Within a few years, we knew we wanted to expand and needed to own the company outright to maintain the quality necessary for the manufacture of our products. We made our Algerian partners an offer, and in June 2010 Dar Al Dawa sold its shares to us for US$18.5 million, making the Algerian plant 100-percent Hikma.

Hikma provides 450 jobs for the community in Algeria and has raised the quality bar for our pharmaceutical competition. It took us two years to improve our production capabilities enough to manufacture our major products there, but the effort's paid off. Algeria has become a good-size market for Hikma. Not only are we ranked second in sales among all the pharmaceutical companies in the country, but we export our products from that facility to clients around the world and collaborate with various international partners, including Japan's Takeda Pharmaceutical Company.

Big Pharma's Diversion Is Hikma's Gain in Tunisia and Morocco

Big Pharma—the large, multinational drug companies—did a lot of merging and consolidating in the beginning of the twenty-first century. That left some of the smaller regional pharmaceutical companies feeling a bit threatened by the sheer enormity of those huge conglomerates.

I didn't see it that way.

I believed the big multinationals would spend most of their resources on research and development, trying to outpace each other in creating new molecules for medications. In order to do that, they'd have to spend less time on manufacturing and marketing—the two important areas where smaller companies such as Hikma could create niches. We took the opportunity to expand our business in less-crowded markets such as North Africa.

We already had a small factory in Tunisia from the early 1990s, when we'd entered a joint venture to gain access there, manufacturing penicillin products for distribution to the French-speaking nations of Northern and Western Africa.

In 2010 we expanded our operations there and acquired a one-third share of Industries Pharmaceutiques Ibn Al Baytar, a pharmaceutical manufacturing and marketing company. A few years after that, Hikma paid US$5 million to buy out shareholders and acquire another one-third of the business. Banks and the Tunisian government own the final third.

We also entered the Moroccan market that year with a majority acquisition of a firm in Casablanca: Promopharm (Société de Promotion Pharmaceutique du Maghreb), which produces products such as eyedrops, effervescents, and a dermatological line.

China and India: Moving into the Largest Countries

It took us a while, but in 2011 we were finally able to move into the two most-populated countries in the world—China and India, giving us access to more than 2.5 billion people and an important foothold in Asia.

First we acquired a significant minority interest in China's Hubei Haosun Pharmaceutical, which develops and manufactures cancer drugs—one of our fields of expertise. Shortly after that we acquired a minority share in Unimark, an active pharmaceutical ingredients (APIs) company in India, which enhanced our research-and-development capabilities. Active pharmaceutical ingredients form the basic core of medicine from which we make other pharmaceutical products.

Competition among pharmaceutical companies in both countries is very strong because of low labor costs, but we're eager to see what additional doors open for us in the future.

Lead by Serving

Less than a year after our new Portuguese plant, Hikma Farmaceutica, became FDA acceptable in 2001, we received a large rush order. A new client in the United States needed five hundred thousand vials of an injectable medication, and they had to have the entire order within two weeks.

Production of the medication wasn't a problem, but packing everything was time consuming. Portugal's general manager at the time, Majda Ladadi (whom I introduced in the last chapter), didn't want to overwhelm the employees in the packaging-and-shipping department, but she also didn't want to disappoint the client or even lose future orders from them by failing to meet their deadline.

Majda decided she and the entire staff needed to come together and help the packaging department. She took a creative and fun approach wherein she led her employees by serving right alongside them. Majda challenged her workers to beat the clock—and the other managers—in a tough but friendly Olympics-style race. The rules were each section would take turns helping the packaging department each day, and the team with the largest number of vials packed would win—along with Hikma and our client.

Employees in the packaging department were sure no one could touch them. Teams from the rest of the plant were equally sure of their abilities and were determined to win.

Competition, done correctly, can be a strong motivator.

First up: Team Management comprised of Majda, her secretary, other executives, and the purchasing manager. They packed twenty thousand vials in one day.

Not to be outdone, the next day the head of the finance department and his staff packed forty-five thousand units.

But it was the technical advisor and his staff who set the record on the third day, packing sixty thousand. They even beat out the packaging department.

Four days later the entire order of five hundred thousand vials had been packed and shipped—one week early.

Majda was following a Hikma corporate tradition of leading her employees by serving them. She rolled up her sleeves and worked right alongside the rest of the staff, helping them to complete their task.

Leadership Means Stepping Down from Your Throne

The most-effective managers are those who can connect with their employees on a personal level, who care about them and their concerns and who resist the urge to flaunt their power. They give direction and lead, but they do so by getting involved and serving those they work with instead of plowing over them with a bulldozer.

Contrast that to managers who feel they're too far above employees even to grace them with conversations and who instead set up walls between them. There's no unity, no sense of team, just a condescending attitude that loudly screams they're better than those with whom they work.

At one US television station a few years ago, the news director ordered her managers, anchors, reporters, and producers not to associate outside of work with the "underlings," or those employees not in management. That's what she called them: *underlings*. Morale was extremely low there, which doesn't surprise me at all. One executive producer even moaned to other producers that it was the most oppressive newsroom in which he'd ever worked.

When one newly hired producer broke the rules and established a friendship with one of the underlings, the haughty news director confronted her about it. The producer defended her actions, saying the underling had been the only one who'd been nice to her when she'd first started at the station.

I can't imagine an executive being so disrespectful in her treatment of her hardworking, minimum-wage employees. Perhaps she'd reached the decision to manage with a superior attitude because she was insecure. But in doing so, she failed see how much those underlings were contributing to the company and what great ideas they had.

When a celebrity's son in another country tragically made news one day, and crews were searching for someone close to the family who could comment on the incident, it was one of those underlings who suggested contacting a local person. It turned out the woman owned a vacation house next door to the celebrity in that foreign country and knew the family very well. No one else had thought of that.

The peon underling came through.

Treat your employees with respect, and never underestimate their abilities to solve some of your company's problems.

Think about Your Employees' Needs

If you don't treat your employees well, they won't be very loyal. Nor will they trust you, and they certainly won't respect you. It's far more productive for a company to have happy, motivated, content employees than those who can't wait to find other jobs and get out as quickly as possible. Workers who feel their bosses appreciate them and their efforts enough to get to know them on a personal level make a positive impact not only in their positions but in the whole company as well.

That's not to say that as a manager, you get soft and put aside your decision-making and other leadership abilities. You can't show partiality toward anyone or become so close you can't correct someone when he or she is veering off course or causing improper conduct at work. But you don't have to be a stone mountain either. You don't always have to be all about the bottom line. Employees are people with emotions and families. Sometimes there are circumstances in their private lives that trouble them so much, they affect their work. As the boss you need to be kind enough to step in, reassure them, and let them know you'll help them through the crisis. They're human. You need to be also.

If you don't care about your employees, you're a terrible leader. Learn to develop compassion for all they're going through while keeping a cool head about the direction your company needs to take.

Employees want to know you're there to listen to them if the need arises both personally and professionally. I'm not talking about people who abuse that and have endless streams of complaints. That's when you need to call in human resources and have them address that. Rather, let your employees know you are approachable if they have concerns or problems.

You can't lead effectively through fear and intimidation. Your employees will never do well if they have to endure that kind of environment each day, and studies confirm that. When people feel their supervisors are threatening them, their job performances suffer.

Serving your employees and caring about them isn't you being weak. In fact it's the ultimate strength. That's what inspires employee loyalty. When you show you sincerely care about them, they'll give their all for their jobs because in return they care about you, want to please you, and don't ever want to disappoint you. And as a bonus, productivity increases.

So does the health of your employees. There's a direct correlation between the way leaders behave and their workers' health, according to a study conducted by Swedish researchers and psychologists at Stressforskningsinstitutet, the Stress Research Institute at Stockholm University. The results of the study, which was published in the *Journal of Occupational and Environmental Medicine* in December 2008, showed male employees were 60 percent more likely to suffer heart attacks or have other cardiac problems if their bosses' behavior created stressful work environments, including if they didn't communicate well or were inconsiderate.

Employees who felt their bosses treated them fairly had a 30 percent lower risk of heart disease, according to a similar study in Britain. And a study in Finland showed workers with good managers had fewer sick days and claimed half as many disability pensions as those whose managers treated them poorly.

Remember: Your Employees Have Families

Sometimes managers or executives spend so much time focused on work and corporate matters, they forget their employees have families who need to spend some quality time with them.

After Said became CEO of Hikma, he and Khalid Nabilis, our CFO and vice president of finance, were traveling through Europe and Britain speaking to current and potential investors in our company. Shortly after they arrived in Scotland, Khalid got a call on his cell phone and, from what Said could hear, it appeared Khalid was going to have to miss an event that was very important to his young son. To some executives it might have seemed minor, but Said knew it mattered to Khalid, and it mattered very much to his little boy.

When Khalid ended his call, Said said, "Let's finish up our meetings today, then I want you to go back to Jordan tomorrow and see your son's school play."

Khalid protested, insisting they had too many important appointments, but Said assured him he could handle them on his own. The next day Khalid's little son looked down from the stage into the audience and saw his daddy sitting there beaming with pride at him and his performance.

Family comes first. Samira and I taught that to Said and all our children as they were growing up, and he obviously learned that lesson well. Khalid, out of loyalty, was willing to make the personal sacrifice of missing an important family event for his other family at Hikma, but thankfully his boss wasn't willing for him to do that.

Said was leading through serving, the way most effective bosses do. Your personal example says so much more than lectures ever could.

Putting family first is one reason why, more than thirty years ago, I decided to establish a free day-care facility for employees' children seven years old and under. That way the employees wouldn't have the personal worries of whether their babysitters were going to show up or even the costs associated with that. And, as an added bonus, the parents could visit their young children on their breaks and spend some time with them in a fun environment.

We're loyal to our employees, and they in turn are loyal to Hikma. Headhunters have contacted Khalid numerous times, trying to lure him away to other companies, but he always tells them he's happy right where he is. And he's not the only one. If your employees are happy, they'll stick with you and your company even through difficult times.

I've always tried to make my employees feel Hikma is theirs— it's their home, and they're my partners. It's not a traditional, hierarchical relationship, and we like it that way. When I started the company, I established a management style that shows appreciation for our employees and lets them know how important they are to our company. That continues to this day. We want to hear what our workers have to say because we respect and value their opinions.

We also don't want them to feel overly stressed about personal matters happening outside Hikma. One day, about ten years after I'd started the company, I noticed our warehouse manager in Jordan was a bit troubled. It turned out he was wrestling with whether to buy an apartment he couldn't really afford. I encouraged him to take it and not worry about the payments. What I knew (and he didn't at the time) was I was about to promote him, and his salary would increase enough to cover his monthly mortgage payments.

However, shortly after that his wife was forced to quit her job to help her family. Since I'd encouraged this employee to buy his apartment, I felt a sense of responsibility and advanced him a check to cover his mortgage that month. I was happy to do it. I was investing in him, and he was investing in our company. He was with Hikma for twenty-six years and rose to become the general manager in Jordan.

Selfish Greed and the Corporate Manager

Some CEOs and heads of companies don't care what happens to their employees. They're selfish and too willing to accept massive layoffs even while they're collecting their hefty paychecks. They put themselves above their companies, their employees, and even their nations in their efforts to make sure they get the largest slices of the pie.

We've seen in the last few years how corruption and greed among CEOs in corporations around the world led to their criminal convictions and either the total destruction of their companies or close to it—well-known names like Allied Irish Banks, Enron, WorldCom, Tyco, Lehman Brothers, Marconi, HealthSouth, Bear Stearns, AIG, Countrywide, Swissair, Royal Ahold, Parmalat, and Bernie Madoff's Ponzi-style investment company.

The West taught me I could attain great heights in business and life, and certainly those greedy executives learned that lesson well. But the Middle East, where I was raised, taught me the importance of community and groups—that a man can benefit others if he climbs to great heights then turns around and helps many more people climb up to join him and share in his success. As my father always told me, it's important to put your employees and partners first, before yourself. You don't get paid until after they get their paychecks. You don't quit for the day and go home until after everyone else has left.

I wish all executives would conduct their businesses that way—that they were honest and fair minded. More managers and business owners need to learn that you have to help people, especially your employees. You don't become so selfish that you step all over them on your climb to the top. And when you get there, don't kick them out of your way or throw them off the mountain.

If lower-level employees are starving or about to be laid off, why are top executives still getting big bonuses in some firms? That needs to stop. Those greedy executives, in my mind, aren't leaders. A leader instills his values and long-term vision in every aspect of the business. What examples are these people teaching other employees? Take the money and run, and forget about the business? No wonder those companies collapsed with "leadership" like that. Many more international corporations need to wake up and realize their leaders are on that same path and may likely suffer the same fate.

Leaders should invest in and care for their employees, not Swiss bank accounts or luxury lifestyles.

Serve Your Community

Because some of our factory employees wear special protective clothing, we're constantly sending out laundry to be cleaned. One day an account manager at Hikma Jordan suggested we buy our own washing machines in order to cut down on the expense. That was certainly a good idea that showed he was thinking about his fellow employees, but he'd failed to realize the impact we have on our surrounding community. By sending our laundry to nearby cleaners and giving them business, we help the local economy.

You should always invest in your community and improve your country in some way. That's something our family believes deeply, and we've always made volunteering part of our lives. For many years Samira has helped women in refugee camps earn money with their crafts and handiwork. She not only buys materials for their sewing and embroidered items but started an organization to market and sell those crafts in Beirut. Samira even handles the marketing and advertising herself.

I carried over what we do in our family to my corporate family. Hikma's always tried to be involved in and give back to communities near our facilities. It's not an official company policy, but it's interesting so many of our employees have personal senses of social responsibility and have always been involved in some sort of philanthropic activities. Maybe that's why we all ended up together in the first place—because we had that desire to help other people. Certainly our business, dealing with pharmaceutical products, involves caring about the health of other people, but our employees around the world make it personal by going out into their communities to get involved in things like raising funds for homeless groups or helping disadvantaged families and the elderly.

So many people were volunteering, and it was such an important part of how we wanted to do business, that in April 2007 my daughter, Hana, our vice president of corporate communications, established our annual Hikma Volunteer Day. The event is designed to give employees from our facilities in Jordan, the United States, Portugal, Saudi Arabia, Egypt, Lebanon, Tunisia, Algeria, Germany, and Italy chances to volunteer and help those less fortunate. More than one thousand of our employees usually take part.

In recent years Hikma Jordan employees visited the SOS Children's Villages, an international organization that helps families care for their children and provides care for children who can't live with their biological families. Our employees helped paint doors and tended the garden then took some of the children on a field trip to the Children's Museum in Amman, where they played with exhibits and did scientific experiments. Hikma's so dedicated to the Children's Museum, we donated money so thirty thousand other students and teachers could get in for free and enjoy the amazing sights and activities it offers.

In past years we've had blood-donation drives and held lectures on topics ranging from proper nutrition to cancer and treatments for it, and some employees have volunteered at the King Hussein Cancer Center Children's Summer Camp. As a pharmaceutical company, we feel a responsibility to support medical communities either by volunteering our time or through charitable donations. We educate and raise awareness and money to help those suffering from diabetes, heart conditions, breast cancer, AIDS, tuberculosis, malaria, and obesity. Hikma also donates medical supplies and oversees their delivery to those needing help in places such as Haiti, Indonesia, Somalia, Libya, and the Gaza Strip.

You're truly the most effective leader when you're serving others.

LESSON FOURTEEN

Control as Much as You Can

I don't like to feel vulnerable either personally or in my business. It's part of my nature as an entrepreneur and an international businessman that I like to control as much of my world as I can. Anything out of control, haphazard, or random has the potential to lead to a multitude of things going wrong.

I don't like it when things go wrong. Some people would call that being a control freak. I call it smart business.

As a manufacturer you're vulnerable to your suppliers and distributors, whose actions affect your cost ratios and timelines. If those outside companies experience shortages or delays, they can cascade onto your company, jeopardizing your production lines and affecting your relationships with your customers by making your products late or too expensive to be competitive in the marketplace.

When you're in the startup phase of your manufacturing process, your company may need to rely on third-party vendors to supply your basic raw materials as well as distribution on the back end, but if you're able financially to assume control of those additional steps, do so. Keep as many functions of your company under your control as possible, so you won't be vulnerable to outside vendors' price hikes, poor quality, shortages, and delays.

That's why, for the sake of quality and our customers, we decided Hikma needed to control more aspects of our production process.

Vertical Integration

For thousands of years, ancient entrepreneurs handled all aspects of their manufacturing from start to finish, or up and down their supply chains—a concept called *vertical integration*. The village tailor and his family may have raised their own sheep to provide wool, which they then dyed and wove into cloth they could design, cut, and sew to make new clothing for other villagers.

But once the Industrial Revolution began in Britain in the late 1700s and early 1800s, times changed. Machines took over many functions people used to do by hand. Combined with new sources of harnessed power such as water, steam, and electricity, the machines provided ways to begin large-scale production of things such as textiles; chemicals like sulphuric acid, alkali, and sodium carbonate; and metals such as iron and steel. The manufacturing of paper, glass, and soap rapidly increased.

As industrialization took off, vertical integration gave way to specialization. More companies and professionals started focusing on niche markets, hiring other firms to supply their materials and deliver their products.

There are a few companies today that still utilize vertical integration. An oil company like BP—which owns the oil wells, the refineries, and the gas stations where the end product reaches customers—is a good example of having complete or balanced vertical integration, meaning the company controls all upstream and downstream aspects of its production process.

There are two other types of vertical integration: backward, where a company manufactures the products used to make its other products, and forward, where a company controls the retail distribution of its manufactured products.

Vertical integration may be a necessity if you're opening a branch of your company overseas, particularly if it's not in a first-world country, and you know you won't be able to count on suppliers to provide needed raw materials.

I decided Hikma would control our production and serve our

customers better if we adopted backward integration by producing our own active pharmaceutical ingredients. APIs are the basic small-molecule, biologically active ingredients used to formulate medications. We need hundreds of them to create our products. By manufacturing our own instead of buying them from other companies, we stood to save a substantial amount.

Initially we started producing the most-expensive APIs and those that were not readily available, which were the most difficult to obtain. By doing that we guaranteed Hikma would always have access to them.

I wouldn't recommend backward, forward, or complete vertical integration if your company doesn't possess the expertise to handle those additional areas well. You don't want to compromise the quality or distribution of your products. Instead consider buying an existing company that provides those materials or services and integrate it into your corporate chain.

Insourcing, Not Outsourcing

Over the years many firms in the West have opted to outsource, or have workers in other countries who aren't their employees do work as subcontractors, usually because the company believes the labor costs are lower than in the host company.

It's always been Hikma's policy to insource rather than outsource for a variety of reasons. Because our employees at each manufacturing plant are primarily from those areas where they work, they're already involved in their local communities and can provide much better sales and customer service and far better quality than a subcontractor in another country with no real interest in our company. And when we don't have to ship as far, we have lower distribution costs.

For instance, the United States is our largest consumer market for pharmaceuticals; our generic sales there account for 40 percent of our profits. Manufacturing the bulk of those pharmaceuticals in another country and shipping them to America wouldn't be cost effective. It's much less expensive to manufacture them near our US clients.

Over the last several years, drug shortages in the United States have nearly tripled, in some cases because the bad economy has forced a number of pharmaceutical manufacturers to reduce or eliminate their production lines. Because Hikma's West-Ward facility is located near major transportation hubs in the New York/ New Jersey area, we've been able to fill those shortage needs readily with affordable, high-quality pharmaceuticals. We wouldn't have been nearly as competitive if we were outsourcing the labor to another country.

I spent years waiting for the opportunity to create a foothold in the esteemed and competitive US market. I feel the greatest pride and honor that we manufacture products there. I challenge American CEOs and entrepreneurs to do the same.

Be Ethical

The foreign-government official smiled slyly after delivering his offer to our Hikma representative. He'd suggested our shipments of pharmaceuticals wouldn't experience any delays if we contributed to his for-profit charity—which was himself.

In other words the official wanted a bribe.

Our Hikma employee smiled back sweetly at the man then informed him that wasn't going to happen on that day or any day. He politely explained to the foreign official that Hikma never gets involved with extortion or the giving or receiving of bribes even if it means the shipments of our products are occasionally delayed.

Sadly, sometimes those delays happen because we won't bend to corruption. It can even cost us market share and profits, but we believe it's more important for us to uphold our good name and a strong code of ethics. Our honest reputation is worth far more than the short-term benefits a few dollars paid as a bribe would possibly give us.

Sometimes the bribery requests have been subtle. Other times they've been pretty blatant. Regardless, Hikma and its employees don't participate. That's our official, set-in-concrete policy. No one gives or gets a bribe. That includes third-party bribes, where corrupt officials may recommend donations to their family members or even their favorite charities.

It's always been my personal policy never to bribe anyone for my own gain or to accept a bribe from someone trying to gain for himself or herself. I established Hikma's ethical code of conduct in the late 1970s, when the company was still in the planning stages, before we'd even poured the foundation of our first manufacturing plant. Those management principles are still printed in our employee handbooks and other publications in addition to being well known throughout the company.

And we've added to them a bit. In 2003 we formally adopted a code of conduct based on Harvard Business School's ethics code, which is a little more detailed and far reaching for global corporations than the one I'd originally designed.

Hikma's ethics code is mandatory for those in management and especially for high-risk employees who are involved in sales and purchasing. They're more likely to come into contact with and have business dealings with corrupt foreign officials. As a publicly traded company, we want our stockholders to know they're investing in a global corporation that conducts business honorably and honestly.

To make sure our employees adhere to our principles, each year we require they read and sign Hikma's ethics code. We make sure each person understands what it means in very specific terms. In addition we've put into place a system of checks and balances to make sure dishonest individuals don't ever have chances to gain footholds in our company or corrupt other employees with their bad behavior. And we provide a way for whistleblowers to report someone's suspected unethical conduct quietly, in order for us to investigate. Employees who are found guilty of deliberately and seriously violating our code of conduct are either laid off or asked to resign.

We've even established a corporate-compliance department whose main focus is to train our employees in anti-bribery and anti-corruption. Our Corporate Responsibility and Ethics Committee, which oversees all ethical issues and makes sure Hikma remains transparent and accountable in all our business dealings, reports directly to our board of directors.

In 2006 we became one of the first one hundred companies to sign the World Economic Forum's Partnering Against Corruption Initiative (PACI), which focuses on anti-bribery and anti-corruption. We're also active members of the United Nations Global Compact and agree to abide by its ten principles, which cover four areas: not indulging in any form of corruption, not being involved in any human-rights abuses, eliminating forced or child labor and any form of discrimination, and protecting the environment while making an effort to go green with technology.

I was raised in a family with great values. From the time my siblings and I were children, my parents always taught us to be honest and humble, and to respect others. Values in the Arab world, for the most part, tend to be based on tradition, and that doesn't change no matter how many decades go by. They're constants that parents instill in subsequent generations, and they aren't easily changed.

I tried to raise my children with the same values my parents had taught me. But I've also tried to teach and instill those values in my corporate employees around the world. I've always wanted them to understand clearly that we don't abandon our principles in order to sell our products.

A company's CEO, and especially his or her values and behavior, sets the tone for how the corporation will do business. If you stick to a code of ethics incorporating honesty, humility, and respect, not only will you be a better person, but your company will build a reputation for integrity, which is as important to your bottom line as your brand.

Managers and company leaders are the role models for their employees. Quality attracts quality. If you're honest, those who work for you will follow your good example. By the same token, if you're dishonest, those employees who are equally dishonest will happily settle into your company and help destroy your business right alongside you, and your ethical employees will soon leave to find better jobs with more-honest employers. Nothing grates on an honest person's conscience like being forced to be around and endure bad behavior each day. In most cases those good, honest employees will soon seek out better work environments and managers who are more in sync with their own values. Iron sharpens iron.

Here's something else to consider: if you establish that dishonesty, and lies are the company norm, then it's a good bet the employees who lie to get business are also lying to you. You'd be foolish to trust them because their only loyalties are to themselves and their bank accounts.

True, you may experience short-term profits if you're dishonest and unethical but only for a while. Eventually it will all catch up with you. If your employees and customers can't trust you, they'll leave. You'll constantly have to be replacing them. That's expensive.

In the long run, you'll be the loser—and you may find yourself looking out of a small prison cell too.

Your good name and the good name of your company are priceless. Don't tarnish either one.

Is Bribery a Business Expense?

Corruption doesn't just line the pockets of a few individuals. Instead it sets a precedent that ultimately destroys lives, companies, and nations. When government officials get in the habit of extracting bribes for services like health care, education, and clean water, it's the poor who suffer the most. They can't afford the extortion, so they end up having to go without basic services. What should be free or affordable suddenly becomes something only the very wealthy can afford.

Corruption and bribery actually increase the cost of doing business—one economic reason to help stamp it out. More important, it's wrong, and in most cases it's illegal and can get you convicted, fined, or possibly even jailed.

For managers and sales associates of many multinational corporations, bribes are business as usual in foreign markets, particularly in underdeveloped countries. Their consciences may bother them a little, and they may not want to do it, but they may believe it's the only option they have. They may sigh as they reluctantly give their authorization, but ultimately they end up adding corruption to their ledgers of expenses for doing business overseas. Prior to 1997 some countries, including Germany and Canada, even allowed corporations to claim bribes as lawful business expenses.

Things have changed a lot in the last sixteen years. In 1997 thirty-four countries that are members of the Organisation for Economic Cooperation and Development signed and agreed to adopt the Anti-Bribery Convention. The document states it's illegal and a criminal act for corporations to bribe foreign public officials. Six nonmember countries have also adopted the convention. That's not a lot when you consider the number of countries in the world, but it's a start. All governments should enact laws and crack down on bribery and corruption.

The global organization Transparency International, in their annual Corruption Perceptions Index, ranks countries according to their levels of public corruption and proclivity to bribery. In 2012 the organization's research revealed the ten most-corrupt countries were Somalia, North Korea, Afghanistan, Sudan, Myanmar, Uzbekistan, Turkmenistan, Iraq, Venezuela, and Haiti. The most disheartening part of Transparency International's research is the revelation that of the 176 countries and territories where its employees collected data, more than two-thirds have serious corruption problems.

The countries found to be the least corrupt were Denmark, Finland, New Zealand, Sweden, Singapore, Switzerland, Australia, Norway, Canada, and The Netherlands.

Interestingly the United States and Britain didn't make the top ten least corrupt, though it wase in the top twenty—just barely.

That said, for American and foreign corporations doing business in the United States, the Foreign Corrupt Practices Act (FCPA) requires all publicly held companies to keep records showing what their expenses are—and those costs of doing business had better not include bribes. Break that law by making any kind of payment to an official in order to get or keep business, and you could be looking at fines in the millions of dollars.

In 1989 the ethics issue hit close to home for Hikma, though it didn't involve our company directly. During the course of investigating the FDA, members of the US Congress unearthed corruption involving approvals of generic drugs. The findings shocked the pharmaceutical industry as well as pharmacists, doctors, and patients.

It all started when a pharmaceutical company in Pittsburgh, Pennsylvania, after launching its own private investigation, filed a discrimination lawsuit against FDA employees and four pharmaceutical companies. The company claimed their repeated requests to manufacture generics were met with constant delays at the FDA because the drug-oversight agency was giving preferential treatment to only a few drug manufacturers.

Three FDA officials eventually pled guilty to accepting bribes, and two pharmaceutical companies pled guilty to paying those bribes. The congressional investigation also brought to light that some generic-drug manufacturers had submitted false records to the FDA. One had even submitted a name-brand blood-pressure drug instead of the generic it was supposed to be manufacturing. In all, thirteen pharmaceutical companies were investigated.

The good thing that came out of the scandal was that the rampant fraud and false claims forced the FDA to establish stricter rules and inspections. Honest companies stayed in business, which made generic drugs safer for consumers, and the dishonest ones were knocked out of the market.

Because of the new higher standards and less competition, we decided to buy a manufacturing facility in the United States—West-Ward.

Do the Right Thing

At Hikma we insist on transparency, which includes proof and documentation for each step in the manufacturing process. We document who controls each logbook and when, how much of an ingredient is added, the temperature of a room, and the results of testing on batches of pharmaceuticals.

Our employees and our customers need to see exactly what they're getting. When you're dealing with medications that affect people's health and lives, you have to do business honestly. Our responsibility doesn't end with our sales to our customers but continues all the way to the patients' taking the medications and getting better.

Since pharmaceuticals are perishable, we make sure our clients understand they need to store our products properly (preferably in cool locations) in order to keep them in good condition, and they must keep an eye on the expiration dates. Most drugs are designed to work only at full potency and are most effective within a set amount of time. Beyond that the chemical compounds can begin to break down. The United States passed a law in 1979 requiring drug manufacturers to stamp expiration dates on their medications for that very reason. If it's past the expiration date, there's no guarantee it will be safe or effective.

When war broke out in Algeria in 1991, many of our physician clients weren't able to store their medications in suitable conditions. In the extreme heat, many of the medications went bad. Even though it wasn't our fault, we sent replacements because we felt our ultimate commitment was to the patients. People will always remember whether you stood with them during a crisis or you abandoned them for a quick sale and short-term profits.

Being transparent is easy when you have nothing to hide. Hikma's always been open and honest with our customers, partners, patients, and stakeholders. Our website, biannual management briefings, quarterly company magazine, and Ask Your CEO initiative provide information about Hikma's short-term and long-term goals, priorities, employee achievements, and answers to questions or concerns.

Doing the right and ethical thing also involves being mindful of our carbon footprint on the environment. We try to operate our manufacturing plants in as green a manner as possible to protect natural resources, which includes looking for ways to reduce carbon emissions better at our plants, taking part in clean-water initiatives by recycling waste water for reuse in our landscaping, and reducing hazardous waste and energy consumption.

Whether you're dealing with foreign government officials, your employees, your customers, or your local communities, make sure you, as a leader, set the standard by being ethical and honest.

Grab Once-in-a-Lifetime Opportunities

I was in Portugal trying to work out some issues at Hikma's newly opened manufacturing plant when an early morning phone call steered my life onto another path.

It was January 1995. A few months earlier, the FDA had reapproved our New Jersey manufacturing facility, West-Ward. It had taken us three years to turn that plant around and correct serious problems we'd found when we'd purchased it, but finally we'd received the OK to start supplying products to the large and lucrative US market.

Hikma was growing quickly—too quickly. A lot of our cash had gone into building our Portugal business from scratch and replacing West-Ward's outdated machinery. Money was tight, which put the company at a critical point. Fewer than two years earlier, I'd told my employees no one was going to be getting a raise for a while.

King Hussein's cousin, Prince Zeid Bin Shaker, who was prime minister of Jordan at the time, chose that moment to phone me. He was a soft-spoken but powerful man, one of the king's closest advisors and confidants. Prince Zeid had previously served as Jordan's prime minister, first in 1989 then from 1991 to 1993. A graduate of Sandhurst Royal Military Academy in Britain and the United States Army Command and General Staff College at Fort Leavenworth, Kansas, he'd also spent twelve years as commander in chief of Jordan's armed forces. Twice he had been made chief of the Royal Court, an administrative group that aids the king and other royals in matters pertaining to the government, the military, and the Jordanian people.

The Hashemite Kingdom of Jordan is a constitutional monarchy. The reigning king is not only the head of state but also chief of the executive branch and commander in chief of all military forces. Until 2013 the constitution stated the king was to appoint his prime minister, who then selected those he believed would be good members to his cabinet, also referred to as the Council of Ministers. (Beginning in 2013 Jordan's parliament took over the job of selecting the prime minister.)

Once the king approves the prime minister's cabinet members, the names go to the legislative branch's lower house of parliament, also called the House of Deputies (Majlis Al-Nuwaab). Jordanians elect those 150 members, of which fifteen are women, nine are Christians, and three either Circassian or Chechen minorities.

The deputies vote whether to approve the prime minister and his cabinet. If the majority votes against the prime minister, he has to resign along with his cabinet.

The other half of the legislative branch is the senate, which is referred to as the House of Notables (Majlis Al-A'yan) or the upper house of parliament. It's made up of sixty senators the king appoints. (The Jordanian constitution states there can't be more senators than half the number of deputies, so there could be as many as seventy-five senators.) Both deputies and senators serve four-year terms.

The third part of the government, the judicial branch, is independent of the executive and legislative branches.

When Sharif Zeid phoned me that January day in 1995, he told me His Majesty King Hussein had just appointed him as Jordan's prime minister for a third time.

"Samih, I'd like to have you in my cabinet, working with King Hussein," he said. "We're forming it right now, and it would be a privilege to have you join us."

I was too stunned to speak. I was a sixty-four-year-old pharmaceutical entrepreneur immersed in business, jetting across continents each week as I tried to find new ways to grow my company and help my customers. I loved helping the people of Jordan in any way I could, but I'd never sought a political office or even considered serving them from a governmental position.

What could I say?

I hesitated as my mind started reeling. Hikma was at such a critical point not only in its growth but also with its cash flow. How could I step away from my company at such an important time in its development?

Yet here was a new challenge, a once-in-a-lifetime opportunity—and I could never resist one of those. Besides that I would be helping King Hussein, a man I greatly admired. From the time he'd first taken the throne in 1952 at the age of sixteen, he'd worked hard to turn Jordan into a strong, literate, and progressive country. He was an intelligent, steady, and immensely important player on the world's stage, a diplomat who was crucial in many negotiations involving the Middle East. How could I say no to my king? On the other hand, how could I walk away from Hikma and all my employees?

"Samih?" Prime Minister Zeid broke my silence. "Will you join us?"

"It would be a privilege to work with you," I said. "I shall be delighted to join your cabinet."

As I hung up the phone, I briefly panicked, thinking about Hikma. Taking this cabinet position meant I wouldn't be able to run the company. Would Hikma survive if I stepped down? How well would my company do without me at the helm? My thirty-seven-year-old son, Said, was the logical choice to replace me as CEO, but I wondered whether he was ready to take over command of all our international operations.

The more I thought about it, the more I realized I'd been preparing him and our employees for this moment for years. Everyone knew his or her job. Hikma was a well-educated and fully trained machine that was absolutely capable of surviving without me. Said knew all aspects of the company, and what small details he didn't know, the rest of our employees did. They'd all be fine.

After sharing the news with Samira, I called Said to tell him he'd just landed one whopper of a promotion.

Two days later I flew to Amman, and King Hussein swore me in as a member of his new cabinet. I'd thought I might become minister of health or minister of labor or education and scientific research, maybe even minister of trade and industry. Instead Prime Minister Zeid thought I'd be most useful to Jordan as the minister of energy and mineral resources.

I'd wanted a challenge, and I'd definitely gotten one.

Evaluating and Grabbing Unique Opportunities

When should you grab an opportunity and maybe even make a career switch that will cause major changes and possibly upheaval in your life?

The answer is as individual as each person. What may be a once-in-a-lifetime opportunity for me may not be for you. And the more people you meet, the more opportunities you'll find coming your way. Like many international executives, I get many offers to serve on boards or join organizations. It's nice to be asked, but I'm selective about the few positions I accept.

In this particular case in 1995, I decided in seconds that performing government service for a country that had given me a home when I was a refugee was motivation enough—even if it meant stepping away from a company I had spent nearly twenty years building and was still trying to build. Jordan had embraced my family and me and provided a hospitable business climate for my entrepreneurial venture. I was more than willing to repay that kindness in any way I could. Besides that, I knew the chance to see how government worked from the inside out was something only a small minority of people in the world ever get. This fascinating new venture was definitely something I didn't want to miss.

When your opportunity comes around, will you recognize it, or are you so immersed in your work you see little else?

Choose to seize the experience if you'll be helping others as well as learning new skills. Take it if it will challenge you to grow as an individual and you'll be working with fascinating people on a daily basis. Grab the opportunity if it's exciting and will never come around again. Jump at the chance if it's something not easily replicated in another outlet or is totally unique and gives you a chance to use some of your strongest skills.

Ask yourself if this new opportunity will benefit or harm your family and you. Accept the new direction only if you're sure you have a backup for your other responsibilities. Do you own a global business or multiple enterprises? Who will take over for you? Are you sure the person is qualified to maintain your company and won't run it into the ground? Do you have a capable board of directors that will make sure the company stays on a steady course? Many presidents and CEOs have stepped away from their companies only to see them collapse in ruins within a few years.

With the position you're being offered, are you willing to be flexible in your new work hours, locations, and manner of operating? Are you willing to go completely out of your comfort zone and start working in a totally unrelated field that forces you to acquire new skills—all without a safety net to catch you if you fail? Are you willing to take the risk? Are you willing to take a pay cut?

More important, are you willing not to be the boss anymore? If you are heading up your own company, are you willing to be subservient to a boss in order to be part of this new experience? If it is a government position, and the officials you work with are unpopular with some of the public, are you strong enough to field criticism and complaints that may be leveled at you?

The Minister of Energy and Mineral Resources

As I had predicted, my time in government service as the minister of energy and mineral resources was very educational and challenging. The challenging part was finding Jordan's natural mineral resources. We didn't have many. Our exploration teams discovered rich veins of granite, marble, and travertine in Southern Jordan, which I had private companies begin excavating and exporting around the world. Those building materials became somewhat profitable, but my major concern was energy.

When I assumed my cabinet post in January 1995, Jordan was importing about 97 percent of its energy needs, including oil. That's true even today, though we're in a slightly better position.

Another problem was Jordan at that time was carefully navigating diplomatic landmines all around us. A few months earlier, in October 1994, King Hussein had signed a peace treaty with Israel, making Jordan the second country to do so following the example of Egypt's Anwar Sadat more than fifteen years prior to that. The treaty King Hussein and Israel's prime minister, Yitzhak Rabin, signed officially ended the war between Jordan and Israel, which had been ongoing since Israel had become a country in 1948. A year before that, the PLO had signed a peace accord with Israel in Washington, DC.

And there were more situations complicating Jordan's interactions with surrounding countries.

Iraq's Saddam Hussein had borrowed $40 billion from Kuwait to fund his war against Iran from 1980 to 1988. When Kuwait refused to forgive the debt, Saddam invaded in August 1990, taking control of the Kuwaiti oil fields. Saddam had also borrowed $26 billion from Saudi Arabia, who refused to forgive the debt as well. After Iraqi forces invaded Kuwait, the Saudis were afraid Saddam's military would cross their shared border and take control of their oil fields too—a move that would have given Iraq control of a majority of the world's oil reserves.

To prevent that, Saudi Arabia joined ten other Arab nations, the United States, Britain, and twenty-one other countries to form a UN-coalition military force to protect their borders and launch an invasion from their country in order to free Kuwait.

Though Jordan is a key ally of the United States and is close to its fellow Arab nations, King Hussein insisted our country remain neutral during that first Gulf War. Throughout, the king maintained close ties with Iraq.

We had to. They were giving us cheap oil.

When the war against Saddam ended in 1991, Jordan was the only country the United Nations legally permitted to receive Iraqi oil (though it was later discovered Saddam had violated the UN economic sanctions and illegally sold oil to other nations, including Syria and Turkey). Jordan was getting half its Iraqi oil free and the other half for a maximum of US$19 per barrel. For a country like ours, which at that time was suffering from high unemployment and importing almost 100 percent of its energy, inexpensive oil was a necessity to keep us up and running.

But as punishment for not joining the UN coalition against Iraq, some Arab countries refused to trade with Jordan or sell us oil or natural gas, including Saudi Arabia.

One of my first goals as minister of energy was to find the Jordanians another source of oil that would be reasonably priced, wouldn't send the country into financial ruin, and would allow us to decrease our dependence on Iraqi oil greatly as we started cutting our ties with Saddam Hussein.

Our neighbors Syria, Iraq, and Saudi Arabia were pumping endless barrels of oil out of the ground each day, and their citizens were benefiting from that, but unfortunately, by some weird quirk of nature, those rich resources seemed to stop at our borders. Even Egypt and Israel had natural gas, but the oil exploration reports up to that time all said there was nothing in Jordan.

I refused to believe that. Conventional wisdom said if there were oil and natural gas deposits throughout the Middle East and all around us, there had to be some in Jordan. We just hadn't found them yet.

I contacted two American oil companies who sent crews to try to find oil, but even though they invested millions of their own money, each time they came up empty or with such small amounts it wouldn't justify the expense of extracting them. However, they did discover a natural-gas field in the eastern desert along our border with Iraq. The Risha gas field isn't large, but it did start supplying about 12 percent of our energy needs.

I knew Jordan needed more natural gas than that, so I approached the Egyptian energy minister about supplying us with their gas and linking us to one of their pipelines. He finally agreed to a fifteen-year deal beginning in 1999, though construction delays prevented the Arab Gas Pipeline from flowing to Jordan until 2003.

That was great for Jordan until the Arab Spring uprisings came to Egypt in 2011 and 2012. At least fifteen times saboteurs blew up the pipeline, which also supplies natural gas to Lebanon, Syria, and Israel. Egyptian authorities claimed Bedouins were responsible for most of the attacks.

The gas pipeline started flowing again on a more regular basis in the early part of 2013, but by then there were gas shortages in Egypt due to the continued uprisings. That meant Jordan received 83 percent less than the amounts agreed to in our contract. Those shortages translated into higher prices for electricity, which, as expected, has been extremely unpopular with the majority of Jordanians.

On top of that, Jordan's free oil from Iraq ended after the Second Gulf War began in 2003. And since the 2012 and 2013 uprisings in Syria, more than half a million refugees have poured into Jordan, increasing our energy demands.

In June 2013 Jordan began importing natural gas from Israel's fields in the Mediterranean, but many Jordanians aren't happy about that because of their longstanding hatred of Jews.

Jordan now spends US$18 billion a year importing energy. The United States and other allies have helped pay some of that, but Jordan's current energy and mineral resources minister, Malek Kabariti, told a conference of Europeans that Jordan's energy situation is, according to an article in the June 18, 2013, *Jordan Times,* "very bad and very serious."

My efforts didn't supply all Jordan needed, but at least I was able to help somewhat in increasing our natural gas supplies with our own reserves and was instrumental in establishing the pipeline with Egypt.

Navigating the Red Tape

As minister of energy, it was good to have the power of the Jordanian government at hand when emergencies arose. When two cars of energy employees took a wrong turn and got lost in the desert one night, it was nice to be able to pick up the phone and contact the Jordanian Air Force to launch a search-and-rescue operation. They found the workers shortly after dawn and led them back onto a main road.

To improve and bring additional electricity to all urban areas, we strung new lines and upgraded the grid (which in later years became interconnected with grids in Lebanon, Palestine, Egypt, Libya, Syria, and Turkey), but in order to reach the most-remote rural and desert citizens, we had to get creative.

Jordan may not have much in the area of fossil fuels, such as oil and natural gas, but we do have sunshine—about 315 days a year. So we installed solar-powered generators to supply electricity to those far away from the main grids and electrical lines and even used them to power wells in the desert that supply water for Bedouin tribes and their camels. Jordanians are beginning to consider solar energy more than they did in the past, but it's still far too underutilized.

We were accomplishing our objectives, though the process was frustratingly slow. The inefficiency of government was more than annoying to deal with on a daily basis. I was used to running a lean, efficient company, but at the ministry we had far too many employees, many of them either duplicating what others were doing or sitting around not accomplishing much at all. The layers and layers of red tape bogged down the whole system, and it moved along at a crawl. It was great so many people had jobs and paychecks for their families, but honestly they weren't necessary. We couldn't dismiss them, so the only thing I could do was try to reassign some of them to other jobs.

In most cases privately owned companies function more efficiently than government agencies. That's because corporations have to improve their products and reduce their prices if they want to become competitive enough to stay in business. That's good for consumers, who end up with better selections at lower costs, but that kind of incentive doesn't exist in government jobs.

I knew my department's government-controlled electrical utility would run more smoothly if private enterprise took over certain functions. But before that happened, the most logical solution was first to organize the utility into three separate functions: generation, transmission, and distribution. To bring about that change, we needed to pass new laws, so I turned to government regulators to help me write a bill for the parliament's consideration. The legislature liked the idea and voted 1996 Decree No (10) into law.

Until then the government-run Jordanian Electricity Authority (JEA) had controlled all aspects of the utility. With the passage of this bill and the Council of Ministers' Resolution of 1997, the electrical utility was divided into the three areas we'd recommended. JEA retained control over the generation and transmission but now allowed privately owned companies to supply some of the distribution. Within three years the JEA was converted into a public company with shareholders, and its name was changed to the National Electricity Power Company (NEPCO).

Today, generation is divided between the government and three privately owned companies, transmission is with the government's publicly owned NEPCO, and distribution is entirely in the hands of three private companies. Eventually the private sector will maintain and run all three divisions of the process. If one company doesn't perform, there will be others to pick up the slack and keep the electricity flowing without interruption, which is good for Jordanians.

What we set up when I was in the cabinet became the foundation upon which following energy ministers have built. We made progress, but we had only about a year to accomplish everything. When I assumed my cabinet post, 87 percent of Jordanian households had electricity. By the time I left fourteen months later, that number had increased to 95 percent. But more than figures on a piece of paper, that number translated into people who had never had access to electricity finally getting it. It changed their lives. We take electricity for granted because it's so basic to our way of life in the twenty-first century, but think about how well you could live without it powering your air conditioning, lights, televisions, refrigerator, stove, microwave, washing machine, and dryer.

Too soon my government service came to an end. Another prime minister was elected to replace Prime Minister Zeid, and a new cabinet replaced us.

Government Service Continues

I thought that was the end of my government service, but three years later, shortly after the death of King Hussein, his son and successor, King Abdullah II, asked me to join his twenty-member Advisory Economic Council, which he'd formed to oversee economic, social, educational, and administrative reforms. I chose to work in the areas of education and health care.

Working with the Department of Education, one of my first tasks was to reform the schoolbooks our students were using. Western writers had authored most of them and included references to obscure things such as fox hunts. We don't have foxes in Jordan. Our students had no idea what they were talking about, nor could they really connect to the subject matter. We replaced those books with ones that referenced our Arab and Jordanian cultures. It's not that we didn't want students exposed to the customs and history of other countries, but we felt it was better, when they were younger, for them to read things they could relate to and were experiencing in their lives.

The second thing we did was implement English-language classes and computer courses for six-year-old students during their first year of school. Then we realized many of the high-school seniors who were about to graduate had never touched computers either, so we immediately began providing classes for them, to ensure they wouldn't go out into the world unprepared.

On the Health Care Committee, I teamed up with physicians, pharmacists, health-care workers, and people in the medical industry to establish quality control in our hospitals. We established an accreditation system in order to guarantee higher standards and requested feedback from physicians. Not only did our efforts result in patient care improving in hospitals, but they inspired Jordanian universities to start offering degreed majors in hospital management.

In 2009, ten years after asking me to serve on his advisory council, King Abdullah asked me to move from the executive branch to the legislative and serve as a senator in parliament. A year later he asked my son, Mazen, to serve as a senator also. Seven years before that, Said had started working for King Abdullah as well. Though we'd never thought of our family as a political one, somehow three of us have ended up in government service—rare opportunities that can come along once in a lifetime.

In 2003 Jordan's prime minister, Faisal al-Fayez, asked Said to serve King Abdullah as the minister of health in his cabinet. The next two prime ministers, Adnan Badran and Marouf Suleiman al-Bakhit, also requested his service in that position. Said held that office for three years, during which time I took over again as CEO and chairman of the Hikma Group. Said left his cabinet post and returned to Hikma in 2006.

Working in government may not be the right move for some people, but for my family, serving our kings, our country, and our fellow Jordanians was an easy decision. The Hashemite Kingdom of Jordan has given us all so much and deeply enriched our lives. We were honored and grateful to be offered such privileges.

Working within a strong government provides you an opportunity to help people in your community and nation the same way working for a solid company does. It also gives you the chance to provide aid to those in neighboring countries. That's especially true during emergencies and crises such as civil unrest, wars, and earthquakes, which is one reason borders should become invisible at those critical times.

That's how Jordan became my family's adopted homeland. We've been proud to serve it ever since.

LESSON SEVENTEEN

Diversify

After leaving the Ministry of Energy and Natural Resources in 1996, I returned to Hikma. Said had handled the company well, but he'd been dealing with the same difficult financial issues that had been there when I'd stepped aside.

There was no denying it—Hikma was on the verge of bankruptcy.

Our sales were strong in America and Portugal and across the Middle East, and we were the largest pharmaceutical manufacturer in Jordan, but all that had translated into higher production costs. On top of that, Saddam Hussein and his Iraqi government hadn't paid us in two years, and our clients in Saudi Arabia weren't paying either. Whatever funds we did get went back into research and development as well as production and expansion.

We had no working capital. Hikma was growing, but we were cash poor.

The main problem was the Jordanian banks. They wouldn't give us loans. From our trying to find funds to build Hikma initially in 1977 to buying West-Ward and building our facility in Portugal, local Jordanian bankers just didn't understand global enterprise and entrepreneurship. They thought Hikma was too much of a risk because we were expanding overseas. That's what a global corporation is supposed to do! They didn't understand because they were too small in their outlooks and attitudes; they were stuck in a way of doing business that had long ago become obsolete.

Because Jordanian banks had refused to give me loans when I'd first started, I'd been forced to find my own capital. It had taken me a year to raise my startup US$1.5 million, and that had included money I'd received from the sale of my pharmacy in Amman as well as investments from my brothers and friends in Jordan.

As Hikma had started expanding, we'd needed more money for new equipment, to hire people, and for training. Again we turned to Jordanian banks for loans, and again they turned us down. They couldn't understand why our facilities needed to be FDA approved.

I felt as if I were banging my head against a brick wall while trying to make these people understand. Attempting to drag these bankers kicking and screaming into the modern world was exhausting and beyond frustrating.

Finally we discovered the International Finance Corporation, the financial arm of the World Bank, which focused exclusively on the private sector in developing countries. They were committed to helping Jordanian industries, and, after sending their team of technical people to our facilities to investigate our operation, they approved our loan for new equipment.

Finally! A financial organization that understood international business. What a refreshing change.

They also gave us a loan to help build our Portuguese facility. We'd timed that one just right because a short while later, Portugal's growth and advancement became so brisk the country was reclassified as "developed," which meant companies there were no longer eligible for IFC aid.

I was so grateful to the IFC and so impressed with the organization, I visited their Washington, DC, offices to meet with the top directors. They told me how pleased they were with the way Hikma was growing.

What saddened and angered me was that the Middle East had no modern Arab banks, only Stone Age ones. Arab companies needed Arab financial institutions that understood and supported their growth, particularly when it came to international expansion—and there weren't any.

"I should start my own bank," I'd mutter to myself each time a Jordanian banker would turn down my request for a loan.

But as the years went by and my frustration grew, that idea started sounding less and less crazy.

So I started my own bank.

Export & Finance Bank

My vision for Hikma has always been focused on the future, looking toward niche markets that aren't being met and areas that haven't been explored. From day one diversification was one of my key growth strategies for our company, but I have to admit I never would have imagined that meant opening our very own bank.

During the 1930s and 1940s, when I was a child and my father owned his own business, most people in Palestine and the Middle East didn't use banks. Merchants usually carried large amounts of cash with them—a highly risky move. I remember my father would help his Jewish and Arab clients cut down on the chances of being robbed by storing their money in his safe overnight while they traveled to buy their seasonal stock. He never charged them interest or levied any other charges on them either. My father was interested only in helping out his friends.

But since those simpler days, the world had sped up to a diz-zying pace and changed enormously. The only thing that hasn't changed is my desire to help other business merchants the same way my father did—and one of those ways was to establish a modern, Arab-owned bank to benefit Middle Eastern businesses.

The first order of business was to educate ourselves about whether we could legally start a bank in Jordan and, if so, what the government regulations were for a venture like that. Once we'd learned it was definitely something we could accomplish, we started mapping out what our new bank would provide.

I knew I wanted it to be not only innovative but, first and foremost, ethical in all its dealings, transparent, and above reproach—the same way I'd set up Hikma.

Even though Hikma was establishing the bank, we had no intention of it being exclusively ours. We wanted to bring quality banking to Jordan to bolster economic growth and elevate industry standards in the Middle East, with an emphasis on full-service corporate and investment banking for our customers. We envisioned a bank that would finance international trade for the business community, trade financial securities on the capital markets, transfer and advance business loans, offer long-term bonds, have a strong financial-research department, and establish a prime-rate concept—none of which existed in the region.

Once we knew what needs we wanted our bank to address, we turned to the difficult task of raising the necessary capital. We needed money not only to build the bank and hire the employees but also to loan our new customers.

Fortunately, at that time we had a representative from Citigroup Venture Capital Equity Partners on Hikma's board of directors, and he helped us with the initial US$28 million funding. We put Ali Husry in charge of the bank's operations, and one of the first things he did was hire the best team of employees he could find.

Our new Export & Finance Bank opened its doors in 1995, and our employees immediately began to help struggling Arab companies find ways to succeed. That has benefited the entire Middle East as well as Hikma. Because of the bank, our company was able to raise the necessary capital to continue our exports.

In a strange twist, as helpful as our Citigroup representative had been in arranging for our initial funding, we soon discovered he didn't have much faith in the longevity of our bank. At one point he advised us to sell Export & Finance Bank and concentrate on our core Hikma business. We politely thanked him for his input but dismissed his suggestion. We had a long-term vision—something he apparently lacked in this one area.

Export & Finance Bank Becomes Capital Bank of Jordan

By 2006 our capital had reached nearly US$164 million, and we were growing at about 27 percent a year. We also were showing a US$28 million yearly profit earned mainly through interest and commissions, and our total assets were US$1.2 billion.

Because we were growing so quickly and adding additional services, we felt the name Export & Finance didn't fully communicate how all-encompassing our services were. So in September 2006, we changed the name of our bank and our logo and officially became Capital Bank of Jordan. Our investment department, which we named Capital Investments, became a separate subsidiary of the bank, handling brokerage services and asset management. We also continued adding branches throughout Jordan and the Middle East.

Be Careful with Your Investors

Capital Bank had been my idea, and I was a major investor, but I hadn't planned to become personally involved. That all changed in September 2009, when the bank's other major shareholders approved a new board of directors and elected me chairman.

Two months earlier the Central Bank of Jordan—our country's monetary authority, which supervises all the banks—became concerned about Hassan Kubba, one of our bank's major investors. He was an Iraqi who had been serving as the chairman of our board for only a few months. We were becoming concerned about him too. Kubba, his father, and their family owned Basra International Bank in Iraq. In February 2006 gunmen dressed as members of the Iraqi Army had kidnapped Kubba and his father, Ghalib, from their home in Basra after killing five of their bodyguards. The kidnappers demanded US$6 million in ransom for the two men, which the Kubbas allegedly paid from their personal funds.

As soon as they were free, Kubba, his family, and the bank's entire board of directors fled to Syria. Kubba eventually moved to Amman and began investing heavily in Capital Bank. In January 2009 he began buying out many of our main Jordanian investors, ending up with a majority 51 percent of Capital Bank. With that he took control of our board and became chairman.

We were stunned by how quickly he'd managed to take control of our bank.

Six months after he'd become chairman, Jordanian government authorities at the Central Bank dissolved Kubba's board of directors and ousted him as chairman, saying they were concerned because he was extending loans to his family and Iraqi business associates even when they didn't have collateral.

Because Capital Bank was so healthy and solid, Jordanian authorities were concerned that Kubba's actions, if left unchecked, would soon destabilize our bank and possibly some of the country's financial community.

We had the same concerns.

Due to pressure from the Central Bank, Kubba reduced his share in our bank from 51 to 30 percent. Our shareholders then elected a new eleven-member board and named me as chairman.

I held the position long enough to restabilize the bank then returned to Hikma.

Capital Bank continued to grow. By 2011 it was the only financial institution in Jordan that provided both commercial and investment banking services; it was also the fourth-largest bank in the country in terms of capital. Two years after that, it became the third-largest bank in Jordan and was named the fastest-growing bank in the region.

My son, Said, is vice president and serves on the board, as does my other son, Mazen, and Ali Husry. Bassem Khalil al-Salem is our executive chairman. Bassem is well qualified for the job; previously he was Jordan's finance minister and chairman of Jordan's Social Security Corporation.

Today our bank's capital is US$232.7 million, with total assets of US$2.26 billion. Capital Bank continues to grow and remains a driving force for socioeconomic development in the Middle East.

Besides that it's a testament to the power of problem solving. No matter who you are, if you see a need in your community or country, try to find an innovative way to fill it yourself. You never know how far you'll grow.

Take Your Company Public

You must have vision and guts if you and your company are going to grow.

I love the Middle East and its people, but they frustrate me at times. Many companies and their owners just aren't future oriented, and they don't believe in long-term planning (something I consider essential). As a result not too many businesses from the Arab world make it to the global level.

Archaic, stuck-in-the-past thinking never grows anything.

I'd rather have 1 percent of a multinational enterprise that helps people all around the world while actively growing and building a future than 100 percent of a small shop that goes nowhere and lazily languishes with zero growth.

But here's a company's catch-22: If you're going to make it onto the world stage, you need to have great employees. And you're probably not going to attract those great employees if you're not a multinational corporation.

So how do you solve that dilemma?

You prove to potential employees you have the vision and drive to steer your corporation into a global marketplace—and show them the company will get there only if they're onboard and helping you.

It's all about your company's employee-talent pool. Employees are the ones who will make or break your company. Yes, they're that important.

Many members of our staff say one reason they joined Hikma was we had the vision to grow beyond the Middle East and take our place in the world marketplace next to Western multinationals and Big Pharma brand-name companies.

Bassam Kanaan, Hikma's president and chief operating officer for the MENA and European Union regions, joined us for that very reason—because we had global vision. Bassam had been born in Jordan, but after graduating from Claremont McKenna College in California in 1986, he chose to stay in the United States because he felt there were more success stories and enterprising role models for him there—things he felt were lacking in his home region of the Middle East.

He started his financial career as an auditor with the prestigious firm of Deloitte Touche Tohmatsu (then called Deloitte & Touche) in Los Angeles, becoming a certified public accountant (CPA) and chartered financial analyst (CFA). After obtaining his executive MBA from Northwestern University in Chicago, he decided to move back to the Middle East to be closer to his family—even though he knew his return to Jordan would probably end all his chances of achieving further career success.

He still had big dreams, so while he worked as CFO for a company in the region, he went back to school and earned his international MBA from Kellogg-Recanati School of Management in Tel Aviv. Now he's president and COO of our international corporation.

It turns out moving back to the Middle East didn't end his career success after all.

Hiring Bassam also helped us achieve an important goal. When he joined our firm in 2001, Hikma was in the early stages of a secret, critically important task—and we immediately put him to work helping us fulfill it.

Charting a Path to Greater Growth

My father always taught me you can't grow and develop by yourself. You need a team of partners and workers.

I knew the only way to achieve our long-term goals and boost our expansion into high gear with access to the largest possible team of investors was to turn Hikma from a privately owned corporation into a public company. For most corporations, the main reason to go public is to have more access to capital for research and development, product-line expansion, and acquisitions. We wanted that, but we also wanted to show our investors we were committed to continuing Hikma's strong corporate governance and consistency.

Plus, I knew that if we raised our level of competition to an international playing field, Hikma would attract an even greater pool of talented employees as well as top global partners. Going public would not only improve our status in the eyes of the world but show the world that Arab-owned companies in the Middle East weren't second class.

In 2000 Hikma Pharmaceuticals was employing more than one thousand people on three continents, and we were expanding throughout the world. Our sales figures were nearly $100 million annually—which was about one thousand times what we'd made in 1979, our first year of business.

I knew the time was right to take Hikma public.

Preparing to Go Public

As any entrepreneur will tell you, the transition from a family business into a publically traded corporation can be extremely difficult to accept. In the Middle East, it's even worse. In Arab culture leaders rarely give up their positions willingly. I thought long and hard about how difficult it would be for our employees and me to begin answering to public shareholders.

After receiving a lot of good counsel, I decided members of our Darwazah family first needed to create Darhold, a privately held company that would allow us to put all our shares under one umbrella. In that way we, as the founders, would retain at least 30 percent of Hikma (Darhold now holds 37 percent). That would allow us to continue to have some level of control and management over the company.

Darhold would also calm international markets by showing

potential shareholders Hikma's originators would still be part of the company, and we wouldn't sell out. We felt it was important for investors to know we were keeping a hand in Hikma, so they would know they could count on the same consistency in quality and corporate responsibility we'd maintained since our company's inception. Going public meant selling shares in our business—not selling out the beliefs upon which I'd based my business.

I called Mohammad Saffouri, one of Hikma's financial experts and a personal friend, to guide us through the process of establishing Darhold. The Darwazahs had been friends with the Saffouri family for years, and Mohammad's father, Mahmoud, had always believed in my vision. He'd become a financial partner in 1991, the same year Mohammad had started working at Hikma, shortly after finishing his bachelor's and master's degrees in finance, management, and budgeting at the University of California and Pepperdine University.

Mohammad helped us set up Darhold, ensuring the company will stay within the Darwazah family for as long as we want to keep it. Darhold gives us a large enough percent of Hikma to guarantee that other shareholders can't do a hostile takeover or sell the company, and it gives our employees a sense of security.

Beginning the IPO Process

At Hikma we always operate on a five-year plan. That's the amount of time it took for us to stop sweating and see our Portugal and US facilities turn around and become profitable, so that's the number I've always used.

I figured it would probably take us five years to get everything in place in advance of launching Hikma on the stock exchange and making an initial public offering (IPO) of stock shares.

Hikma had a decentralized structure, with no one team monitoring all our facilities from a unified corporate perspective. We knew if we were going to go public, we had to start centralizing everything and get the right team of professionals in place.

That first year we focused on attracting talent to Hikma, especially in the area of finance. One of our most important hires was Bassam Kanaan, whom I just mentioned. He reorganized our company, prepared the teams we needed to be ready for outside investments, and started putting together a fiscal plan. He also improved our financial reports and made sure our internal control systems were in line with international regulations, so Hikma would be as transparent as possible for shareholders once we did go public. Along with that we established a decision-making structure of checks and balances, so we could quickly detect anything fraudulent.

Next we met with advisory teams from Citigroup, Merrill Lynch, and Credit Suisse. They suggested we bring in a private-equity party in order to gain more access to capital because the biggest drive for investment in an initial public offering is a company's ability to grow.

We still hadn't decided where we would go public. Initially we considered the New York Stock Exchange. The manufacture of generic drugs was still relatively new in most of the world, but in the United States, which had the largest pharmaceuticals market and where we did 50 percent of our business, there were already strong generic companies. Investors there would be familiar with what we did. That made New York seem like the best place to launch.

Then, suddenly, things changed.

When the TYCO and Enron scandals hit America, the US Congress began introducing tough new laws such as the Sarbanes-Oxley Act, which required companies to produce more-detailed internal control records. We realized a small company like Hikma wouldn't be able to handle the expense associated with implementing that kind of system.

We started looking more closely at the London Stock Exchange, another important hub for financial investors interested in emerging markets and international funds. One benefit was Britain had more straightforward and fewer detail-oriented laws than the United States and required less documentation and bureaucracy. Another benefit was the United Kingdom was one of the main entries into Europe and closer to the MENA region, where our business was steadily increasing.

After consulting with our advisors, accountants, and lawyers (who handled our corporate tax issues), it became clear our IPO needed to be on the London exchange. In early 2004 we started the process in earnest, with October 2005 as our target date to go public.

We assembled Hikma's top management and mapped out what we needed to accomplish in the next eighteen months, including compiling information about major agreements and financials for the lawyers, accountants, and advisors as well as producing monthly and quarterly accounts.

We appointed a project manager and a team from each subsidiary to draft a strategic business plan and complete an analysis of each of our company's facilities in terms of sales, profits, and performance. In the summer of 2005, just a few months before the launch of our IPO, we met again in London to present a plan for expanding business in the United States and MENA markets and to report on our current and projected financials. That became the basis for our presentation to potential investors.

In more than fifteen meetings held over two weeks, Bassam, two members of our executive staff, and I tried to convince investors to come onboard with Hikma. We focused on our US generics and our branded business in MENA as well as the quality and reputation of our injectables.

Even though it was an exhausting two weeks, I was determined to set an example for my three young colleagues. I woke up early each day and was the first person in the car. In the evenings, when we'd finally get to our hotel, the other three team members would want to go to their rooms immediately to rest, but I always insisted we have dinner together first. Relaxing over a good meal strengthened our team and gave us the energy we needed for the next day's investor meetings.

Hikma Goes Public

On November 1, 2005, the day of our initial public offering, conditional offers of Hikma Pharmaceutical shares were taken, and we had what's called a *book-running process*: our Merrill Lynch advisor called all the potential investors we'd met to find out what they were willing to invest in Hikma—a figure that would determine the median price of our stock.

A *conditional* offer is when someone will go through with their purchase of shares only if certain conditions are met. Once those conditions have been met, the offer becomes *unconditional*.

We ended up with three times more subscribers than we needed. Merrill Lynch sponsored our listing, and Citigroup acted as the joint lead manager with them, along with Hikma's Export & Finance Bank (now Capital Bank). We became the very first Jordanian company and the first Middle Eastern pharmaceutical company ever to be listed on the London Stock Exchange.

Three days later, on November 4, unconditional offers were taken.

On our initial public offering, 166.5 million shares of Hikma stock at 290 pence (GB£2.9) per share were issued. Since then our stock has delivered a shareholder return of 191 percent and now sells for about GB£10.05 per share (US$16.31). Many of those 2005 IPO investors still hold shares in our company.

With our infusion of cash from the sale of public shares, we've been able to acquire more pharmaceutical companies, notably in Saudi Arabia, Jordan (APM), Egypt, and Germany, as I mentioned in earlier chapters. We've also caught the eyes of some multinational corporations that expressed interests in partnering with us in areas such as biotechnology.

We've accelerated our sales and reached a higher level of profits. Now Hikma has facilities on four continents and the goal of expanding into even more of the most-competitive and burgeoning world markets. While several Western and global stalwarts have fallen due to mismanagement, greed, or complacency, our revenues have broken the US$1 billion mark.

We have more access to capital for growth (most of which comes from shareholders in the United States and Europe) and can find large outside investors and bank support. Hikma is better recognized by many financial institutions, which helps with future research and innovation. When we announce our intention to make an acquisition, we've already got the cash for it lined up from investors.

It's a big change from the early days, when we were so cash poor.

Going Public Brings Changes

The initial public offering certainly paid off in terms of growth, but going from an entrepreneurial private company to a publicly traded one certainly brought some changes and adjustments.

One main area was the form of governance. Before, whenever I wanted to start working on a new project, I'd just do it. My personal rule was never to go public with a plan or project before it was completed.

That's all changed. Now we have to announce any changes, plans, or potential acquisitions at an early stage. That's not all bad because it forces us to follow through on our announcements and achieve both our short- and long-term goals, but it's a big change in the way we have to work.

We've retained our same policies and haven't lost our overall sense of the Hikma family culture, but now everything's on a larger scale. When we were a private entrepreneurship, there was more focus on employees' individual accountability and personal achievements, but now we have to be more numbers oriented to show our shareholders how successful we are.

We've had to change our procedures a bit to meet public and government regulations, which brings more paperwork and record keeping, and hire more consultants to tell us how to act upon the many codes of governance. That's because being listed on the London Stock Exchange means we're required to report to an external agency in Britain that verifies our business practices and level of corporate responsibility.

We decided we wanted Hikma not only to comply with regulations but to go above and beyond. That's why we've chosen to adhere voluntarily to global reporting indicators, a corporate report card that 80 percent of multinationals use. The indicators measure our revenues, costs, donations, and investments; how we benefit the public; our rates of worker injury, disease, lost days, and absenteeism; the average hours of training we give each employee; our anticorruption policies; how much energy and water we use; our total weight of waste; the impact of our handling and shipping; whether our suppliers and contractors respect human rights; and how well we discover, disclose, and decrease any harmful effects of our company.

We've had to increase our legal department to deal with these new government and international rules and regulations. We used to have one lawyer; now there are dozens. Our financial department is larger to deal with our increased operational costs, fees, taxes, and shipping costs. Plus our record keeping for finances has to be available for any investor who asks about sales and accounts—though that's something we were always open about anyway.

Adding new systems to track financial matters has been very beneficial. When our financial department switched over to our new documenting system prior to the IPO, the staff was surprised to see exactly how much we were donating to charities and contributing to our employees' benefits, including food (free meals at work), education, health care, and Social Security. Even if we have a facility in a country that doesn't require health care or Social Security, our policy has always been to provide those services for our employees.

Prior to the IPO, we started a corporate responsibility program through my daughter Hana's communications department. Through that new program, we introduced an official Hikma code of conduct and established a board-level steering committee and an expanded working committee. Each year we hold a human-resources and corporate-responsibility training workshop in Amman, which our employees from all over the world attend.

In 2006 Said completed his government service in the Ministry of Health, and he returned as CEO in July 2007. I stayed on in my capacity as nonexecutive chairman of the board.

Our board of directors has grown in size. It now includes Hikma's nonexecutive chairman and founder (me); my two sons, Said and Mazen; and Ali Husry. It also includes four independent directors from outside the company who are experts in business, pharmaceuticals, accounting, and finance: Sir David Rowe-Ham, a former lord mayor of London and executive with Lloyds Bank who's well versed in financial matters, corporate governance, and public affairs; Michael Ashton, an Australian who's held senior executive positions with Pfizer and Merck pharmaceuticals; Breffni Byrne, an accountant from Ireland who's been a managing partner with the renowned financial firm Arthur Andersen; and Ronald Goode, an American who's served as president of international operations at Searle and vice president at Pfizer Pharmaceuticals.

There have been some arguments—the eight of us don't agree on the definition of *football* or who has a better team—but we do agree on Hikma's goals of growth, research, and innovation. The board meets eight times a year in London and once a year at one of Hikma's international facilities.

How Going Public Affected Our Employees

Our employees have adapted well to be being part of a publicly traded company. In fact they're enormously proud of it. They knew going public would help not only our company but the countries we were in through employment, exportation, an influx of foreign currency, and an increased company profile. Our employees were enormously helpful in the years leading up to the IPO and in the transition.

"I had emotional feelings and thoughts about achieving an IPO," Dr. Othman Abu Gheida, our director of MENA human resources, wrote to me in a letter. "I feel very proud of Hikma and its people and our future. We proved we can be equal to the best of the breed worldwide. During my adult life, I felt we in the Middle East were not always progressing and were perhaps sometimes going backward in some ways. Hikma's progress is a rare experience that needs to be advertised and multiplied."

Our talented people are still able to work in creative and innovative environments, but Hikma is now rapidly moving forward, which means we have to be careful in selecting the right person for each job. Employees not only have to fit into Hikma's corporate culture; they also have to maintain the level of efficiency our customers and investors have come to expect.

Before the IPO Hikma usually promoted and developed from within. Our employees still have ample opportunities for promotion, but now, because in-depth, on-the-job training isn't always practical, we're hiring more people from outside the company who already have the skills to match our specific needs.

Employees can still apply to further their educations, but the system's a little different from prior to the IPO. Before, the staff members in human resources would have approached each employee individually, but now they send out mass e-mails informing workers they have to apply for education funding. The results are the same, but the system's changed.

We've created new full-time staff positions that handle social, health, and environmental issues in all our main manufacturing facilities. Before the IPO these were just practices; now they're policies. We've always bent over backward to meet our employees' needs and help serve the communities where we have facilities, but we didn't have many clear-cut, official procedures until we went public. By institutionalizing such practices, Hikma has been able to keep good people—and, more importantly, make their lives even better.

We've attracted a lot of new, talented employees, but sadly we've also lost a few. Our system of giving employees shares in Hikma was designed to retain and reward our loyal staff, but some chose to cash out, leave the company, and take their money to pursue other interests or early retirement.

An Example for Others

As Dr. Gheida wrote so well, Hikma has become an example for others in the Middle East. If we could start a small company in a small country with very limited resources and become one of the fastest-growing multinational corporations, even cracking the highly competitive American and European markets, others can do it too. Hikma is a clear example that any company, no matter where it's located, can reach its goals.

You aren't limited by your location—only by a lack of vision.

We've had our share of doubters along the way, saying, "You'll never grow," "You have too many competitors," and "You won't succeed in that market." Frankly, the facts were on their sides. Very few family companies anywhere in the world—and very few Middle Eastern companies, family owned or otherwise—become successful, publicly traded corporations.

I know the main reason Hikma became successful—besides having wonderful employees—is we looked to the US business model of success and adopted it while still retaining the good, strong qualities of our Arab culture.

Find Something Positive in Every Nonvictory

I slowly opened one eye as a loudly crowing rooster, perched a few feet away from me, gave me my early morning wakeup call. Suddenly I felt something sharply jab my head then pull my hair. As I reached up to rub the spot, another sharp jab hit my hand. Fully awake now, I looked around to see a group of chickens all around my bed, pecking at it and me in their search for food.

Welcome to downtown Mukalla, Yemen.

It was the early 1970s, and I was on a business trip for Eli Lilly, staying at one of the town's few "hotels." Since the inn's owner had said he didn't have an air-conditioned room for me, he'd graciously offered me a cot in the fresh air—on the building's roof—where I could take advantage of the cool breezes.

He'd failed to tell me the roof came with roommates.

When I complained to him about the chickens, he promised to keep them out of my "bedroom." The next morning I awoke to find a goat staring at me as he munched on my luggage. Obviously this was my fault since I'd failed to specify I didn't want *any* barnyard roommates.

Going to Mukalla was not one of my better ideas. In fact it was pretty much a failure. My boss in Rome had told me it was a crazy idea and had tried to talk me out of it. He'd warned me it wouldn't be a fruitful sales call, but a man who owned a small drugstore in Mukalla had begged me to come, promising he'd be my distribution agent in the area.

The Yemeni town had once been an important port for British ships traveling to India, but when the ships stopped coming, it turned into a ghost town. In fact I found illustrations of Mukalla from 110 years earlier, and the place looked exactly the same.

After the druggist gave me an order worth a few thousand dollars, I tried to beat it out of town only to discover the creaky DC-3 that was scheduled to fly me to the port of Aden was delayed—for two more days. Or maybe three. Maybe more.

As informative as the trip to Yemen was, and as interesting as it was to travel to Mukalla, I learned I should have listened to my boss.

Victory Won't Always Be Yours

You're not going to win every time.

Though it's nice to imagine your every brainstorm will be a profitable goldmine, the reality is sometimes things don't quite work out as you'd planned.

But that's OK. Failure is educational, and there's always something positive you can take away from the situation. Sometimes you learn more from not winning. It can teach you to look for better ways to overcome the obstacles that possibly prevented your victory in the first place.

No matter what your business, you're going to experience your share of setbacks. The key is using those failures as opportunities to do better.

Our first product line at Hikma started with four items: two antibiotics, one anti-inflammatory, and one medication for pain. But the anti-inflammatory never made it to market because I couldn't convince my sales team it was a better choice than what was already available. They didn't want to waste their time trying to promote something they knew wouldn't sell.

That wasn't my only pharmaceutical failure. We started manufacturing a product called Doloflex, which was a combination of two of our extremely effective products: a relaxant and a pain reliever. Unfortunately the two didn't work together. The drug was a dud, and we immediately withdrew it from the market. That taught me to test every possible combination of a product before launching it. The lesson was invaluable.

In the late 1990s, we came up with another product that didn't do well: a chewable antibiotic for children. It tasted great, but when we put it on the market it was a complete disaster. The reason? Apparently parents want their children's medicine to taste terrible. They're convinced medicine is only effective when their sons and daughters make gagging faces as they take it.

Again it brought me back to the all-important practice of market research. Test every product before you put it on the market.

Then there was my heritage misjudgment. When I'd first started Hikma, I had assumed the Arab world and governments in the Middle East would support my endeavor. I was establishing a good, honest pharmaceutical company that would help people and bring employment to the area, and I expected my fellow Arabs to recognize that. They didn't. I quickly learned people don't care what you're doing unless they have personal stakes in your business.

That's an important lesson for entrepreneurs, and it was a good one for me. No one's going to take you by the hand and pull you up. You have to depend on yourself and those closest to you. Trust me, that's usually all you need.

Then there was the friend misjudgment. I learned quickly that just because I knew someone, that didn't mean he or she was going to support me in my business—even if it would help his or her own business. I had a very good physician friend I thought would be one of the first to buy my pharmaceuticals. To my amazement he didn't. I had to persuade him strongly just like I would have any other customer. That taught me that connections, friends, and networking are useful tools to open doors, but you still have to find a way to walk through them and close the sale.

I learned another nonvictory lesson when Hikma was listed on a second stock exchange. We went public on the London Stock Exchange in November 2005, then we decided to do a listing on the Dubai International Financial Exchange (DIFX) five months later. On April 26, 2006, we listed our global depository receipts (GDR) with each representing two ordinary shares.

Our listing in London had been a huge success. Dubai? Not so much.

While we were doing our research as we prepared to go public, Dubai's economy was soaring, with no signs of slowing down. But shortly after we listed on the DIFX, the global recession hit hard, and Dubai's economy tanked.

I took away two lessons from that: even the most researched, analyzed, and calculated risk is still a risk, and you should always stick to successful markets.

You Win Some, You Lose Some

One day in late 2006, two representatives from Ernst & Young came to my office in Amman. Ernst & Young is a large corporation started in 1849 and headquartered in London; it offers accounting, investing, and financial services at its many offices around the world. In 2012 *Forbes* magazine ranked the company as the best accounting firm to work for. A few years earlier, *BusinessWeek* had ranked it as the best place to launch a career, and *Fortune* magazine ranked it as one of the top one hundred best companies to work for.

Each year Ernst & Young selects local and global entrepreneurs of the year. The representatives told me 2007 was the first year they were holding the competition in the Middle East. They said it was a developing, fertile area for entrepreneurs who had enough courage (and funding) to act on their visions.

I thought they were inviting me as a guest to the event, but it turned out they'd come to tell me I was a nominee. A group of business tycoons and investors would act as judges and select the final winner.

The three-day ceremony began in Dubai on February 20, 2007. I immediately recognized the well-known businesspeople surrounding me; they headed up some of the largest multinational corporations in the Arab world. The majority of the nominees came from the Persian Gulf countries of Kuwait, Oman, Dubai,

Abu Dhabi, Bahrain, and Saudi Arabia, and their accomplishments had been well publicized in the regional and international media. These large corporations had long tables full of guests—quite a contrast to our table. Hikma was the smallest company there.

First the judges explained their process in choosing the entrepreneur of the year. They had looked at the risks and amount of capital each entrepreneur had when starting his or her business, and they were most impressed with those who had started with small investments but managed to grow into corporations making national and global impacts.

I'd started my company with only about US$1.5 million and wondered if anyone else had opened their doors with less than that.

The judges also had taken into consideration which leaders had high standards, strong values, corporate responsibility, willingness to take high risks, track records of persevering as they overcame obstacles, innovative and pioneering approaches to business, visions for future growth, and the ability to put together strong teams of employees.

Then they announced the winner of the Ernst & Young 2007 Entrepreneur of the Year for the Middle East award...and it was me! The judges had selected Hikma. I'm sure everyone in the room was as surprised as I was.

My win automatically put me in the running to become the 2008 global entrepreneur of the year. My family and I traveled to Monte Carlo for that ceremony. I didn't win (the judges selected a biotech expert from Switzerland), but it didn't matter. We had a wonderful time meeting my fellow regional winners and enjoying a few days in one of the most beautiful cities in Europe. No one really came away a loser.

We may have lost that award, but we still had a lot of wins in our future. The next year in London, Hikma received the 2009 SCRIP Intelligence Best Company in an Emerging Market award. We were honored to have this recognition of our excellent performance.

The lesson learned is this: you're going to win some things, and you're going to lose others even when you're doing a quality job and putting all you've got into it. Just remember not to get discouraged if you don't always end up victorious because there's a good chance you have a win coming in your future, maybe just around the corner. Whether you win or lose, the experience is always a great learning opportunity—and your journey can turn out to be a lot of fun.

Anticipate Future Trends

"Can you help us?" the young woman asked me timidly. Penelope Shihab had put everything into her dream company, MonoJo Biotech. She had overcome almost insurmountable obstacles, including obtaining the initial financial backing for her startup. It was hard enough for technology entrepreneurs to grow their companies in the Middle East; it was even more difficult if the founder and CEO happened to be a woman. Penelope owned the only biotech company in Jordan, and I admired her greatly for coming as far as she had.

Biotechnology is the process of creating products from living organisms, usually for medicine or food production, but in the last few decades it's also been used to create diagnostic tests, to analyze genomes through DNA sequencing, and to manipulate our immune systems to fight diseases more effectively.

Penelope had earned her bachelor's degree in medical biotechnology from Applied Science Private University in Amman and, in September 2005, had started MonoJo Biotech as a research arm affiliated with six universities. But two years later, she'd run out of money and was on the verge of shutting down.

That was when she approached me for advice about how to save her company.

I digested all she told me and slowly shook my head. I knew I could turn her company around and give it a future, but it wasn't going to be easy.

I like challenges, and this was definitely going to be one because in the two years MonoJo had been in business, Penelope and her staff hadn't brought a single product to market. They had nothing to sell. How did they expect to make money? By continually asking people to donate for research? That would never do.

I told Penelope I'd be willing to help her if she'd let me invest an amount equal to what she'd initially raised as capital when she'd started. That would give me a majority share in her company. But for that to happen, I told her, she'd have to make me executive chairman of the board and let me take over MonoJo.

I had no plans to make this company a Hikma subsidiary. Instead I wanted to do this on my own, to invest in MonoJo personally—a side project of sorts.

Penelope immediately accepted my offer but told me MonoJo had no board of directors. That needed to change immediately.

Some of her major shareholders included the head of the biotech department at the University of Cambridge in England, the CEO of Infinity, and members of a French biotech company, so I asked them, along with a few others, to make up the new MonoJo board. Next I checked the staff's qualifications. Penelope was very active, energetic, and knowledgeable, a key person in the company, but most of the other scientists were working only part time. To me that meant they didn't have fully vested interests in the company.

Not only that but they were imitating the research on genetic diagnostic products and procedures that other companies had already done and brought to market. MonoJo wasn't competitive with any company; they weren't producing anything innovative, and they weren't making any money.

We offered one of the scientists a promotion to technical director then asked him, the general manager, and the other scientists to come up with ideas for new research subjects that could be sold to make money. I also asked a few people at the Jordanian universities affiliated with the company to come up with useful things MonoJo could produce, with an emphasis on products or services that would be good for Jordan's technical advancement.

When the projects came in, we selected a few of the most innovative and useful then began hiring more scientists. We also hired four camels—not just because they're a familiar sight throughout Jordan but because they were going to be key in our first commercial venture. We extracted antibodies from the camels' milk for pharmaceutical purposes, mainly as a remedy for gastrointestinal problems, and used proteins from the milk for a highly commercial idea we had.

Our research and testing had indicated the camel-milk proteins could be used very effectively in high-end cosmetic and skin products, such as acne cream, anti-wrinkle cream, moisturizer, and sunscreen. It took more than five years of testing and development, but our scientists have created a line of products with antimicrobial properties, which we've named Skinue. We planned to launch the products in the United States in late 2013 or early 2014.

Our Jordan MonoJo facility now does contract-research work for other companies, which is bringing in some revenue, and in 2012 we opened a branch of the company called Columbia Biotech in the United States, at the University of Missouri Columbia. Penelope is managing both the Missouri and the Jordanian locations as well as raising four children and completing her PhD at Cambridge. She's a busy woman.

We also created a nonprofit division of MonoJo called Applied Scientific Research Fund (ASRF), which is dedicated to the support and patenting of new inventions in the fields of engineering, information technology, medicine, and applied science. The profits from ASRF go back into the company to help fund ecosystem innovations and sustainability in Jordan and the Middle East.

We're just getting started, but we're always looking to the future. Fortunately we have a great staff, and that's our best resource. We've given the MonoJo and ASRF employees the freedom to be creative, and they've risen to the challenge.

Finding Future Trends

Some things from our childhoods always stay with us. Many times they're lessons we've learned through hardship and heartache.

When my father lost all his property in Palestine, leaving my family practically destitute, that experience stayed with me. It taught me always to look forward and try to control the future the best I can, but then that's the nature of entrepreneurs. We plan ahead and use our ideas to try to change imperfect realities to more closely resemble our somewhat-more-perfect visions.

One of the best ways I know to change the world is to create new industries while adding value to and improving existing technologies. Biotechnology, along with continued research, is taking the pharmaceutical industry into the future, and that's one reason I enthusiastically got involved with MonoJo and ASRF.

Biotechnology includes the use of biomarkers, or substances that are introduced into the body then traced to determine if there's organ function, if an infection has progressed, or if a disease is responding to a treatment. Biomarkers are used in clinical trials during the first stages of research to determine how effective pharmaceuticals are. Biotechnology is getting better at targeting specific forms of disease, and that's leading the way to more-customized medicine.

Because biotech involves the replication of molecules, even minor differences or inconsistencies can lead to big differences in the quality of products. That's why conditions have to be so precise. Using biotech requires a strong commitment to clinical research—something Hikma continues to believe in and support. We put a large percent of our sales back into research and development. That's why Hikma became the primary investor in a clinical-research center in Amman called International Pharmacy Research Center (IPRC), which Dr. Naji Najib started in 1997.

Dr. Najib had received his degrees in pharmacy in Britain then did postdoctoral research in the United States and was a Fulbright scientist there. Later he became dean of the school of pharmacy at Jordan University of Science and Technology.

IPRC provides research for the pharmaceutical industry and has conducted more than eight hundred studies and clinical trials for the MENA region, Europe, and the United States.

Through IPRC, Hikma has developed more than 140 of our own products. Our return on investment is in lives saved, not just profits earned. You can't reap the benefits of a world market without shouldering your share of the responsibility for the populations you serve. When new, innovative medication was developed for the treatment of HIV and introduced to our North African markets, AIDS-related deaths dropped dramatically.

In contrast, many of our competitors, particularly the major multinational pharmaceutical firms, have been getting away from research because of budget restrictions and huge overhead costs. That means fewer new products. Instead Big Pharma tends to focus more on aggressively marketing their recognized, name-brand products.

The Future of Pharmaceuticals

Generic pharmaceutical sales from companies such as Hikma are continuing to grow, substantially outpacing brand-name products. One reason for that is health-care costs are too high in developed countries such as the United States, and generics offer alternatives to expensive prescription and brand-name drugs. Another reason is the middle class is growing in emerging markets like China and several MENA countries, and they want more access to pharmaceutical care.

The global generics market was estimated to be worth about US$225 billion in 2011. It's expected to rise to more than US$350 billion by 2016, showing a healthy increase of almost 10 percent in five years' time—higher than projections for brand-name pharmaceuticals. Generic sales are also rising because new markets are opening up in emerging areas, such as India, parts of Eastern Europe (especially Russia), and countries such as Mexico and Brazil. Sales are small compared to those in the United States, Western Europe, and Japan, but generics will most likely drive the future growth in those emerging markets.

Generic sales are rising at a fast rate in developed, first-world nations even during economic downturns. In fact that's the very time when many people turn to lower-cost alternatives such as generic drugs to save money. Generics offer the same quality for much less—sometimes 90 percent less. That's why governments and health-insurance companies are on the side of generics: because it's cheaper for them to cover the costs.

Even those who have good health insurance will pay about US$40 a month for a brand-name cholesterol drug. The generic version for the same month's supply is only ten dollars and is just as effective. Some of the most-expensive but most-used drugs on the market cost three to five dollars per pill, so imagine how much that adds up for someone who has to take them once or twice a day.

And imagine the profits Big Pharma companies make off those drugs. Today the sales of name-brand drugs reach almost $300 billion annually in the United States alone.

How did the costs get so high? Pharmaceutical companies that manufacture those name-brand drugs claim they have to charge higher prices to recoup the hundreds of millions of dollars they've spent on research and development. Add to that the costs of advertising and promotion, and you can see why name brands cost more than the comparable generic drugs.

Those Big Pharma companies know that many generic pharmaceuticals are exactly the same as theirs in terms of quality and effectiveness—and more consumers are realizing that too. Generic companies use the same active ingredients as name-brand drugs and have to undergo the same strict FDA or federal testing, so the safety and effectiveness of generics is ensured. Only the price is less, and the brand name is missing.

The number of generic drugs will continue to grow as Big Pharma's patents on well-known, brand-name drugs expire in the near future (something CEOs of generic companies refer to as "the day I've been waiting for all my life"). Once the patents expire, generic manufacturers can begin replicating the drugs and selling them at much lower costs.

Six of the ten best-selling, name-brand drugs in America (sometimes referred to as *blockbuster* drugs) are going to lose their patents soon. That includes one for diabetes and one for high cholesterol—two medical conditions that are on the rise in the United

States. Some brand-name companies are positioning themselves for that day by starting their own generic manufacturing divisions or partnering with existing generic companies.

Planning for the Future

I'm a compulsive planner. I can't do a project today without taking into consideration the future possibilities. What should our strategy be for the next three to five years? Which countries? Which products? How can we upgrade our skills to keep pace with the company's growth?

We encourage our Hikma employees always to plan ahead, with agendas for daily, weekly, monthly, and three-year to five-year goals.

One of the best ways to plan is on paper because it makes you consider all the aspects and strategies you'll need to implement to achieve your goals and make them real. If you don't plan, your expectations will probably be higher than what you can achieve in the short term, and that can lead to failure.

Hikma's short-term goal was to be a billion-dollar company by 2012, which we achieved. Our long-term goal is to reach the US$5 billion mark by 2020, which is not impossible since we've doubled our sales every four years.

In addition Hikma's strategies for continued growth include strengthening our leading presence in the MENA region, where the pharmaceutical market continues to grow at a pace well above the global average, and expanding further into the large Egyptian market; growing our core business in the United States; and continuing to make acquisitions and start greenfield projects. We also plan to invest in sales and marketing to maintain our strong market position (our products are sold to chain stores, wholesalers, distributors, health systems, hospitals, and governmental agencies); develop new products in therapeutic areas of research; partner with other companies to help launch products; and increase our worldwide production capabilities.

We don't plan to sell Hikma. It's just not an option. And we've set up a system to guarantee there won't be a hostile takeover, sei-zure, or acquisition of our shares for at least fifty years.

We might consider a partnership or merger if we think it would increase our technological capabilities and introduce us to new markets such as Japan, Eastern Europe, South America, and Australia.

The growing shift toward generic pharmaceuticals shows people want high-quality, innovative products that are accessible and affordable. That's what Hikma will continue to provide.

That's our future.

LESSON TWENTY-ONE

Stay Close to Your Family

I gazed out at the deep-purple sky, the music from the orchestra soaring and blending with the operatic voices of the cast. More than 3,200 of us were enjoying another night of the annual two-month-long Puccini Festival at the Gran Teatro all'Aperto (an open-air theater) in the small, picturesque Tuscan town of Torre del Lago. Just behind the stage, a full moon rose over Lake Massaciuccoli, its reflected light shimmering over the water as a soft breeze blew.

Even better than the beauty of that moment was having my wife, children, and grandchildren there with me.

Ciao bella.

I wait all year for this. Each August, Samira, my children, their families, and I return to Italy for our annual vacation. It's a time for all of us to be together, relaxing and having fun as one big (and ever-growing) Darwazah clan.

There's a reason we always make Italy the reunion destination: when my wife, four children, and I lived in Rome during my years with Eli Lilly, we fell in love with the Italian people, the stunning scenery, the fabulous food, and the amazing culture. Italy will always be a special place for us. Our roots and happy memories go as deeply into Italian soil as they do into Jordanian sand. And now another generation, my grandchildren, have fallen in love with Italy too.

When we first started going for our August vacations, we'd rent a small house. That grew to two houses as May, Said, Mazen, and Hana started marrying and having children. Then, as more grandchildren came along, and they started marrying, there were so many of us the only place large enough was the entire floor of a hotel.

What surprises me is the amount of excitement every member of my family feels about this annual reunion. My eleven grand-children are scattered all around the world in their careers and in school, but they consider this family time together so important, they put everything else aside. They save their vacation time specifically for this trip. Some of them say they've looked forward to it each year for as long as they can remember. Imagine teenagers actually wanting to spend time with their parents, grandparents, aunts, uncles, and cousins.

No matter how hard they work and how focused they are on their careers and schooling, they've learned how important it is to stay close to their family.

Put Family First

Whether you're starting a company, already have an established and growing corporation, or are just launching your career, you never seem to have enough hours in the day. No matter how you plan, you're probably constantly finding you don't have enough time to accomplish all you'd like. To accommodate your work schedule, you may sacrifice other areas of your life—like your family. Don't do that. Don't ignore your spouse, children, and parents, hoping you can catch up in later years. Those years may never come, or you may end up so estranged from your family that when you finally decide you have the time, they may not want to make time for you.

My wife and children have always been part of my schedule. I've always tried to make sure I spend as much time as possible with them, even when my travel and business obligations threaten to keep me away for days at a time. I always have lunch with Samira when we're in the same city, and if we're not, I phone her to talk about everything.

I admit it's partially selfish. I need my family. I must have them always in my life. They keep me centered and remind me what's really important. Even when I was worrying about Hikma's bottom line, Samira, my children, and my grandchildren kept me focused on the bigger picture—and they still do. Family is always more important than your career, your business, or your corporation.

When Samira and I were first starting out as a married couple, we were so fortunate to have family members helping us. Because we didn't have a lot of money, both of us had to work outside the home even after baby May came along. We wouldn't have been able to manage if our family hadn't helped us. Relatives would come and stay for months at a time to help care for our little daughter while Samira and I were working.

But staying close to your family means much more than just having free childcare. Your family reminds you who you are, what your roots are, and from where you came. They teach you how to make your way in the world and give you invaluable advice. Children learn to socialize and communicate first in a family environment. That's where they obtain their code of ethics and learn to have respect for other people and to share. Family provides the secure base and safety net you need in order to launch out into the world with courage and confidence in ever-bigger ventures. Your family loves you unconditionally like no one else ever will. Everyone needs that.

Samira and I knew how important it was for our children to learn how to make decisions on their own, so we showed them good examples of ethics and morals, taught them what the consequences of wrong actions would be, then sent them out into the world. We always made sure to let them know we were still there, and they could always come to us for advice or help if they needed it. However, we wanted them to grow up and learn that their parents weren't always going to be there to make decisions for them. They had to learn how to navigate this world on their own, independently, without being reckless and foolish.

They had to grow up.

My four children quickly discovered that with the freedom

to make their own decisions came a heavy sense of responsibility. They knew their mother and I trusted them. Because of that, and because they knew our expectations of them were high, they always tried to do their best and not do anything that would disappoint us. The trust and freedom we gave them helped them develop the confidence they needed to spread their wings.

It falls to the older generations to nurture independence and innovation in children and grandchildren.

Despite my background as a teacher and my role as public speaker, I don't like to give lectures. I've always believed the best way for parents to teach their children and grandchildren is by example and with a heavy dose of encouragement. If you lecture an audience, they may walk out. If you lecture your children, they may rebel. But if you show your morals through the way you act and the way you live your life, those values will make an unforgettable impact on other people.

Actions speak loudly whether it's teaching morals and ethics or giving encouragement.

When my grandchildren were younger, if they'd toddle over to show me proudly their latest crayon or colored-pencil artistic masterpiece, I'd say, "What a pretty picture. Draw me another one, please." When they did I'd either have the picture framed to hang on our wall, or I'd post it on my refrigerator.

Positive reinforcement gives children the confidence to chase their dreams as they get older. When one of our granddaughters was in school, she was doing extremely well in her English and history classes but was struggling in science and math. She came to me, clearly disappointed by those grades. But I took a look at them, considered the situation, and told her, "You've done well in English and history. Both of those require a lot of studying and critical thought. Anyone who does well in those two subjects certainly can apply the same skills to do well in everything else."

I wanted to encourage her in the areas where she was doing really well. That way she'd find a way to improve in her weaker areas.

Whether it's encouragement or teaching manners, your example speaks loudly to others. One night Samira and I were at a restaurant for dinner with our daughters and a few of their children. We were expecting two other guests, but they were running late and hadn't arrived. Everyone had had a busy day, and we were all extremely hungry. But while my grandchildren quickly dug into the appetizers, I decided to wait and not eat until our guests arrived, so they wouldn't be eating alone. I also wanted to show my grandchildren how to have patience as well as how to respect others enough to put them before themselves.

As soon as my family noticed I wasn't eating, they all stopped eating too and patiently waited for our guests. I'd communicated the right thing to do through my example, not through lecturing.

That doesn't mean I don't talk to my family. To the contrary I believe maintaining close family relationships is a necessity, and communication is the best tool. Whether it's in person, on the phone, over Skype, or via e-mail or texting, you need to stay in touch with your family.

I always want to be in touch with my wife, children, and grandchildren, but I want them to be in regular communication with each other too. Mazen and Said travel around the world regularly for work, but whenever I speak to either of them, I always make sure to ask, "Are you keeping in touch with your brother?" They ask me the same thing about my brother, Mohammed, the philosopher of the family, who's still successfully running the business our father started.

Even though Mazen and his wife are in Jordan, and their son, Tareq, is working in New Jersey, Tareq still calls them each day for a thirty-minute conversation. He stays in touch because he values their wisdom.

A few years ago, I e-mailed my grandchildren, who were scattered around the globe at various universities and jobs, and requested they all sign up for the BlackBerry Messenger service so we could all keep in better touch with each other. I told them if anyone didn't have a BlackBerry, I'd provide one. The next day they all got together via BlackBerry for a "cousin conference," messaging each other about where they were and what they were doing.

When Said's daughter, Yasmine, traveled to Boston, Massachusetts, in 2011 to tour the campus of Babson College and decide if she wanted to attend there, she got in touch with her cousin Walid, Mazen's son. He'd just graduated from Babson and happily dropped by the campus to give her a tour of his alma mater. That sealed Yasmine's decision. Walid was such a good guide, she's now attending Babson.

The bond between family is the strongest glue on Earth. It can't be broken. But it's up to every member to maintain the quality and closeness of those relationships with each other no matter how large or small the family.

Stay close to your family. They won't be around for ever. Neither will you. Enjoy the time together whenever you can find it.

Have Fun Together as a Family

Loving your family and communicating with them are essential, but it's also important to have fun together. Those relaxed moments will create memories that will last for decades. They also encourage a lot of personal growth in children, who are always trying to mimic whatever their parents, older siblings, and cousins are doing.

When we're in Italy, we rent bikes and cruise the streets together. When some of the grandchildren were too young to ride, the adults would attach kiddie passenger seats to their bikes so the little ones could ride with them. Most of my grandchildren enjoyed those carefree, early years of riding behind their parents, taking in the views without having to work their little feet to keep the bikes moving. But at least one of them didn't like being singled out as the baby of the family.

When my youngest grandchild—Shareef, Said's son—was

only three years old, he decided he wanted to be like the big kids and ride a bike all by himself. The problem was he didn't know how, and his parents thought he was still too young to learn. Even though he was still a toddler, Shareef borrowed one of the other children's smaller bikes each evening for a few hours and taught himself to ride it—without any of us adults finding out. I'm sure a lot of falling down was involved, but Shareef persisted. A few days later, he proudly demonstrated to all of us how well he could ride and keep pace with the group. To say his parents and grandparents were surprised (and very pleased) is an understatement.

To Samira, as proud as she was, Shareef was demonstrating some of his grandfather's stubbornness—with a head so hard he almost didn't need a bike helmet. I saw it differently. To me, Shareef, even at that early age, was showing a budding entrepreneurial spirit (as well as athletic talent and a great sense of balance). He found a way to solve his problem, he overcame the obstacles, and he achieved success on his own. That took bravery, optimism, innovation, and independence—all qualities I like to find in the leaders of my company and hope to see in future generations in the Middle East.

Like Shareef, all my children and grandchildren have been bold and fearless about trying new things even if they occasionally fall and scrape their knees. I've always encouraged them to learn new things no matter how difficult or controversial they may be, to push themselves to do more, learn more, travel more, take on ever-bolder challenges, and keep their minds open to different cultures. I'm glad to see they continue to challenge themselves and persevere as they push forward to achieve their goals and dreams.

Group activities with the whole family are always fun, but it's also important to spend one-on-one time with your children and grandchildren in order to develop and maintain close individual relationships. It's important to let everyone know how truly unique and special he or she is to you and to create memories just the two of you share.

During one of our vacations in Italy, I asked Hana's daughter, Tamara, to sign up for a wind sailing class with me. I wanted her to join me for a fun event, but I also wanted her to see there are always ways to challenge yourself and learn something even on a family holiday.

Tamara's pretty adventurous, and she enthusiastically agreed to go with me, mistakenly thinking it would be a light, beach-type activity. Instead it turned to be serious basic sailing instruction for beginners.

I was the oldest one in the class, and Tamara was the youngest, but our team was definitely the best. Together we tied knots, controlled the mast, and learned to sail. We had a lot of fun too, and we both have great memories of that special time with each other.

A while ago May's daughter, Deema, reminded me of the time we were together off the coast of Italy, on a paddleboat in the Tyrrhenian Sea. I inhaled deeply and told Deema to do the same because the air was so fresh and clean, the moment so peaceful, and the view so spectacular. I wanted her to learn to enjoy each moment and the small things in life, which can bring us so much pleasure. Deema says now that every time she's by the sea or in the mountains, she takes a deep breath of fresh air as a reminder of that wonderful moment when we were together.

What makes this story even more special is Deema e-mailed me that memory while she was on her honeymoon. I'd asked all my grandchildren to think of some stories for this book, and Deema took the time away from her new husband to share the memories of our time together that are so important to her. Memories like that are precious.

Love your family members, and stay close to each one of them. They'll make you a better person.

Watch Your Health

Samira and I could see the rain falling on Manhattan outside the window of the doctor's office. It certainly matched our moods. We were both nervous, waiting to hear the results of the tests I'd recently taken.

This specialist was the last in a long line of doctors I'd seen over the course of a few months. All the others had said my tests were negative and nothing was wrong, but if that were the case, why was I still feeling pain in my abdomen?

It was 1999, and Samira and I were living in a small apartment we'd purchased in Cascais, just outside Lisbon. FDA officials had begun their inspection of Hikma Farmaceutica a few years earlier, but it hadn't been approved yet. I wanted to be there in Portugal, close to the plant, to make sure everything involved with that process stayed on track.

We'd traveled to the United States to visit this particular specialist because something told me the other doctors and their diagnoses were all wrong.

I was right.

The New York doctor had done an endoscopy and discovered a small mass in my colon. He'd sent it to be analyzed, and on that rainy August day, Samira and I anxiously waited to hear the results.

After greeting us, the doctor got right to the point. "I'm sorry, Mr. Darwazah," he said. "You do have cancer of the colon."

The news hit me so hard, I found it difficult to take a breath.

"The good news," he continued, "is that we've caught the disease early. It should still be treatable."

My family was devastated, particularly because it was the second time cancer had hit us that year. Said's wife, Mami, had been diagnosed and treated a few months earlier.

Having worked in the medical and pharmaceutical field for so many years, I didn't give in to despair but instead began searching for more information. My research revealed colon cancer is usually hereditary. My older brother had had it, which meant one of my parents might have unknowingly had it too.

For someone with a strong family history of colon cancer, screening should begin at the age of forty—specifically, four times during your forties, five times in your fifties, six times in your sixties, and once a year after that. Early detection can mean the difference between life and death.

I wanted to receive treatment as soon as possible. I'd already lost months because of the other doctors' wrong diagnoses. Mami had just been treated in the United States, and I knew that was where the best treatment was. I selected St. Luke's Hospital in New York City after learning it had the top colon-cancer specialists on staff. On September 2 I had surgery there to remove the small mass.

Fortunately the cancer was localized and hadn't spread, which meant I didn't need chemotherapy or radiation treatment.

Eat Well

My doctors in New York recommended changes in my diet and lifestyle, which I willingly accepted. As part of the global pharmaceutical industry, Hikma and our products help sick people heal, but that doesn't mean I believe we should all rely solely on pills and medical treatments to keep us healthy.

Some diseases are hereditary, but far too many are the results of our abusing our bodies or, at the very least, not taking good care of them. Hundreds of millions (if not billions) of people in developing, third-world countries come down with a host of diseases and illnesses because they don't get enough of the proper foods to eat; ironically that's also a contributor to diseases in first-world nations. Food may be more abundant in developed countries, but that doesn't mean it's of high quality. Far too many people don't eat enough good food.

Years ago I'd hoped the world would learn enough about some of the most-prevalent chronic diseases—such as diabetes, cancer, lung infections, and heart problems—to eliminate them, but instead the number of casualties they claim rises each year. That's why I'm always encouraging Hikma employees to become leaders in health themselves. We, of all people, need to set an example of good health. Because we're so committed to our employees' welfare and well being, we regularly schedule forums for them that give important pointers about healthy nutrition and lifestyles. We also encourage disease prevention by providing our staff with free services like mammograms.

One of the first keys to good health is putting good fuel into your body. That may sound simplistic, but in first-world countries, where so many people work long hours at their jobs, home-cooked, healthy food has given way to eat-on-the-run, microwaved prepared meals; donuts from the conference room; multiple bags of highly processed products that drop down from vending machines; or fast-food hamburgers with greasy French fries and sugary drinks.

It's no wonder so many people are overweight and ill.

One of the worst offenders is processed sugar, which is added to everything from cereals, coffee creamers, and soft drinks (twelve teaspoons in each can) to ketchup, salad dressings, and even healthy-sounding items like soy milk and almond milk. That's in addition to the endless variety of cupcakes, ice creams, cookies, pies, and cakes tempting us on a daily basis. People in first-world countries consume as much 140 pounds of sugar a year. Our bodies can't handle that.

Is it any wonder so many people are being diagnosed with diabetes at increasingly earlier ages—even when they have no history of diabetes in their families? If you dump four to five teaspoons of sugar into a cup of coffee three times a day for twenty or thirty years, it doesn't take a doctor to tell you you're probably going to become diabetic.

In February 2010 Dr. Mehmet Oz, the vice chair and professor of surgery at Columbia University in New York, an author, and a well-known television personality, wrote an article for the *Huffington Post* website detailing the harm sugar does to our bodies. Dr. Oz, a cardiothoracic surgeon, said he's operated on thousands of patients whose hearts were destroyed by diabetes. That's because when your body can no longer metabolize sugar, it floats in your bloodstream and becomes like "shards of glass scraping the inner lining of your arteries," according to Dr. Oz. He said when those scrapes heal, they leave behind scar tissue that causes blockages, resulting in heart attacks and strokes. The sugar shards can also damage your kidneys so badly, you wind up on dialysis.

Ninety percent of diabetics are type 2, which means they weren't born with the disease, and it's not hereditary. They acquired it.

The good news is you can prevent type 2 diabetes, and even if you're showing symptoms you can reverse them with the proper diet. Avoid sugar and its substitutes, like high-fructose corn syrup. If you really feel you can't live without something sweet, get it naturally by eating fruit.

A basic rule for good eating is: the closer a food is to its natural state, the better it is for you. Conversely, the more processed the food, the more empty calories and the less nutrition it has.

The use of pesticides on crops has grown over the decades in an effort to increase yields, but our bodies aren't processing those harmful chemicals well. Nor are we able to absorb the abundance of hormones and antibiotics found in our meats, eggs, and dairy products. For healthier eating, you might consider switching to organic foods, which don't have antibiotics, hormones, and pesticides.

As the founder of a pharmaceutical corporation, I know how necessary and important antibiotics are. They help kill off harmful bacteria and save people's lives. But they're also in many of our foods and overused for minor illnesses, too frequently administered when they shouldn't be. That's because when bacteria survive a round of antibiotics, their genes form a resistance to that particular medication. Eventually bacteria mutate to form strains that are resistant to *all* antibiotics and become what's classified as *superbugs*. There are no cures for them.

Not only is the overuse of antibiotics giving rise to new strains of superbugs, but it's also causing damage to our bodies. We each have on average more than one hundred trillion good bacteria in our intestines. Those good bacteria help keep us healthy. In fact many experts say 80 percent of our health begins in our intestines.

But an antibiotic doesn't distinguish between good and bad bacteria. It kills them both. That means if you've taken a round of antibiotics, or you're eating foods that contain them, you need to find a way to restore your good bacteria by increasing your intake of yogurt (make sure it's without sugar) or by taking a probiotic on a regular basis.

The CDC warns doctors to prescribe antibiotics only when they're absolutely necessary and advises patients to stop demanding them every time they come down with the least little sniffle or cough.

Of course the other health suggestions are: eat lots of fruits and vegetables while making sure you still get enough protein in your diet, avoid smoking, limit your intake of alcohol, and regularly exercise to keep your heart healthy.

The Cancer Returns

My colon cancer led me to discover more about not only the disease but the medications being used to treat it. I started looking at oncology products and decided they should be available everywhere and at affordable prices. That's one reason Hikma's research and development department began creating generic forms of some of the most commonly used oncology medications.

I'd received a clean bill of health after my 1999 colon surgery, but in 2013 the cancer returned—this time as lymphoma, a type of blood cancer. Doctors discovered it after I came down with pneumonia in March and ended up in the hospital for tests and treatment. I started chemotherapy right away and received six treatments over the course of four months. Fortunately my last treatment was a month before our annual Darwazah vacation in Italy, so I was able to join my family—surely some of the best medicine I could have had.

Know When to Step Aside

There should come a time when your company has become well established enough that you can safely and confidently step aside. If you've prepared your successors well, you shouldn't worry. But that's the key: you need to take the time to groom the person who will head up your company after you carefully.

From the time I'd started Hikma, I had planned for it to continue without my leadership. I had no desire to govern the company as my private fiefdom forever. Instead I worked to make sure Hikma would be a viable, self-sustaining corporation—one that would provide help to patients around the world and employment to citizens of different countries for generations to come—even long after I left. Your legacy shouldn't be you; it should be your family and the company you've built as well as the values you've left with all of them.

Can your business survive without you? Will there ever be a time when you can step down from your position as CEO? How well have you prepared the next generation to step into your shoes? Many a corporation has failed when the founder died or stepped aside, leaving it in the hands of those who couldn't maintain the momentum and didn't have the same vision to keep it growing.

I knew my son, Said, would take over for me. After he'd received the proper education then shown the necessary skills and successes at Hikma, I knew he was more than ready to begin his preparation for the day when the company would rest solidly on his shoulders.

He hasn't disappointed me.

That's not to say his brother, Mazen, as well as May, Hana, and the other executives, the members of the Hikma board, and our worldwide employees aren't equally important to the success of the company, but I trained Said to step into my shoes. As I write this in the fall of 2013, Said's been running Hikma for six years. In 2007 I stepped down as CEO and began serving as the board's nonexecutive chairman. Now it's up to Said to identify and train his successor, preparing that person for the day when he decides to step aside too.

Said's been exploring many new directions for growth, and his leadership has been giving Hikma a new energy. That's exciting for me to witness. He has the same long-term vision and strategic thinking I do, but we have slightly different ways of implementing them, and honestly his ideas are better than mine.

I'm more impatient than he is, so that always factored into my strategy. Once I'd done my research, I quickly moved to acquire companies in bad shape then turned them around in about three or four years. If I couldn't get a company quickly, I wasn't interested and moved on to something else.

Said's more reflective than I am. He takes more time to analyze a situation, but his thoughtfulness has actually led to faster growth. He takes his time looking for good grassroots companies then comes alongside them and starts with them on the ground floor. The result is Said's been able to achieve faster growth for Hikma than I ever did.

Starting New Ventures

Playing endless rounds of golf was never my idea of the perfect retirement. I'd be bored out of my mind. Instead of retiring I started acquiring new businesses. That's typical of most entrepreneurs. We can't sit still. We need to find new challenges and problems to solve. If we wanted easy lives, we wouldn't have become entrepreneurs.

In 2008 I purchased Labatec Pharma, a small, family owned company in Geneva, Switzerland, that had been founded in 1957. It was manufacturing oral tablets and capsules. My research revealed the Swiss generic-drug market was growing at a brisk rate, but there were only two or three existing generic competitors to fill that need. I realized Labatec could offer the Swiss medical community high-quality generics at tremendous savings. We could sell our products for more-reasonable prices than in other European countries while still keeping the costs well below those of Big Pharma's name brands.

I knew I had to bring in a few key people to get the company running in the direction I wanted. In May 2008 I hired George Dabit from Hikma to work as my marketing director and general manager. George had received his bachelor's in business administration from my alma mater, American University of Beirut, and his MBA in management and marketing from the University of North Carolina's Belk College of Business.

He was working as a strategic planning and development manager at Hikma in Jordan when I lured him to Switzerland. Actually I borrowed him for three years to get Labatec up and running; Said wanted him back in 2011, so I reluctantly returned him. (Muriel Xatard, who'd been Labatec's quality manager since October 2009, then took over as director of operations.) George is now in charge of writing bids as Hikma's tender director in the MENA region.

George was invaluable in helping me establish the new direction for Labatec. As soon as he came onboard, the two of us realized the company needed a new operating system to guarantee any personality changes wouldn't affect the way the company functioned—something you have to consider when you're switching over from a family owned business.

The simplest way to get that kind of structure in place was to set up an IT system. George and I decided to develop one based on the Sage-3 model we were using then at Hikma Farmaceutica in Portugal. We contacted the system's manufacturer to find out how to replicate it in Geneva then looked for someone to install the software. We ended up hiring Miguel, an enthusiastic and talented young industrial engineer from Portugal who had experience with that particular IT system.

While Miguel worked on our system, George and I started reviewing Labatec's employees in manufacturing, marketing, operations systems, and finance to figure out who was a good fit in each position. I also started formulating our marketing plan while deciding which products we'd offer. My research showed Switzerland needed more suppliers of injectables, so I added those to our Labatec product line.

Everything with my new acquisition seemed to be running smoothly.

Too smoothly.

Miguel finally got our new IT system up and running after long hours and a lot of hard work. As he proudly demonstrated it to George and me, he said, "It's so simple. You just push this button, and…"

Nothing happened.

George and I stared at the blank computer screen where our bank account, inventory, cash flow, and sales were supposed to be. Miguel had done a great job with the software system—except he'd forgotten to save all the information he'd entered.

I had thought things were going a little too smoothly.

Miguel went back to square one with Labatec's IT department while George and I started registering thirty of our pharmaceuticals. Registering is a tedious and time-consuming process, but it's a necessity if you want to get your products on the market. The information you have to include for each drug on a certificate of pharmaceutical product (CPP) includes: the name and number of the drug; the exporting, or certifying, country, which in this case was Switzerland; and the importing country. That means if we're shipping a product to various countries, we have to do a separate certificate for each country that will be importing the pharmaceutical. Also listed on the CPP is the drug's composition (the active ingredients); the dosage; the licensing information; what kind of marketing presence we have in our exporting country; and the details of our company.

We estimated it would take us about five years from the time we started registering Labatec's thirty products to the time we were approved and received the registrations. I'm too impatient for that. To speed up the process, we decided to divide the work and outsource part of the registration to consultants in Germany, Switzerland, and other European nations. Labatec handled the majority of the drugs. Because we divided the workload, we completed the application for the registration of our thirty products within one year and received registration approval for twenty-seven of them within two years—record time in the world of pharmaceuticals.

By the summer of 2010, we'd finished building a refrigerated room to store our injectables, and Labatec's products were on the market, much to the surprise of our competitors. Their reactions were swift. One of the larger pharmaceutical companies—the originator of a brand-name product we offered in a generic version for much less money—lowered their price to twenty-five francs. We then lowered our price to seventeen. When they went down to twelve and a half francs, I contacted their CEO and told him we'd chase them down as low as they wanted to go—and then we'd go even lower.

He knew we'd beaten them. We weren't in it to make an immediate profit. We wanted to gain clients for Labatec and have our products recognized. If we practically had to give away our generics to get people to try them, that's what we were prepared to do.

In March 2009 I hired François Détraz to be Labatec's sales director. He and his team started contacting physicians and hospitals throughout Switzerland to introduce them to our generics. However, changing from one pharmaceutical manufacturer to another is never an easy decision, especially for large medical centers.

One hospital director was particularly reluctant to switch to us because of the sudden plunge in prices that had occurred after we'd burst onto the market. His facility had been using the name-brand originator drug, and if the Big Pharma supplier were dropping their price, he felt a loyalty to stay with that company.

I love a good challenge, so I decided to drop in on the director for a visit.

"You should thank me," I told him. "We're the reason you're paying lower prices."

The director carefully listened to what I had to say then decided to give us a chance by splitting his order fifty-fifty between Labatec and the name-brand originator. It didn't take him long to recognize Labatec's quality after using the two products during the same period and comparing them side by side. Our service, as well as our attention to his needs and concerns, also impressed him.

The next time his hospital needed more of that particular drug, he gave Labatec his entire order. One-third of the hospitals in Switzerland are now Labatec clients.

The Meaning of Success

I went from being a refugee in exile to owning a successful global enterprise, from having no home to owning homes on several continents.

People are always wondering about the secret to success, as if there were any one such thing. Hard work, the right timing, a clear plan, enough funds, having a good product, luck, and family support are all important in succeeding as an entrepreneur.

But most of all, you must have passion in all areas of life. That's not the secret to success—that's the definition of it.

You have to be passionate about your company and your products but also about your employees, your customers, and the communities you serve around the world. You have to care about the people who make your products as well as the ones who use them.

Wanting success for its own sake is never enough. You must have worthy goals and take pride in what you do. Trust me, that's far more important than making large profits. Even though money was definitely an issue, we never concentrated on that as the number-one priority. From the time I started Hikma, I've tried to build a company that would not only help others who are sick but help build up each region where we have a manufacturing facility.

Here's the payoff: if you really care about people and have worthy goals, the money will come—along with your contentment. But if you seek only money, you probably won't find it, nor will you find happiness or success.

Individuals Need Recognition

Whether it's a family, a corporation, a country, or the world, we need to adopt a team attitude without sacrificing the achievements of individuals. Work together in unity, but don't forget about each person.

That last part's very important, and yes, it's a Western approach. The Arab world tends not to elevate the individual above the group. Though it sounds noble, that approach can slow down independent thinking and innovation.

I hope that changes.

Our ancient Arab culture has many traditions and values that should be respected and passed down through the generations. As a business leader and an Arab, I've always wanted to show the world how people in the Middle East have integrity, vision, a strong work ethic, compassion, humility, and hope.

But we need to grow too. The Middle East needs new technology, progress, and advanced societies. And we need to recognize, celebrate, and acknowledge individuals for their hard work and outstanding achievements. Along with financial incentives, people need personal recognition for what they do. Their successes need to be celebrated and acknowledged.

Parting Thoughts

As long as I'm capable, I'll continue to work. I'll also continue to have lunch with Samira every day. I can't see any sense in giving up either one of my two passions.

My family used to encourage me to relax and retire, but they've finally stopped nagging me. Frankly I haven't really worked since

I started Hikma. Like they say, choose a job you love, and you'll never work a day in your life.

I've always loved going to the factory to see my employees whether it was 6:00 a.m. or midnight. I used to know everyone personally, but Hikma's too big now. We have thousands of employees spread out over many facilities in numerous countries on multiple continents.

Since stepping down from my position as Hikma's CEO, I've learned to relax a little and not interfere in the daily running of the business. I'm satisfied because I see good results, and I know the company couldn't be in better hands.

No matter how large it grows, Hikma is still a family business based on family values from the first generation of my parents to the current fourth generation of my grandchildren. Hopefully the company will still be around for their children's grandchildren. I couldn't imagine having a better succession plan in place.

Even though I'd love for my talented and resourceful grand-children to want to work for Hikma and keep it in the family, I don't want them to choose that path if it's not what they want. I want them to go where their skills and talents lead them even if it's in a completely different direction. Three or four of them are already showing interest in entrepreneurship, and I'm encour-aging them to start planning for their own businesses if that's where their passions lie. I tell my grandchildren they will succeed if they act with passion, purpose, and focus, but the best way I can teach them is through my own example.

I hope I've inspired my children and grandchildren. My parents were my inspirations and role models. There's something to be said for the wisdom and experience that comes from our elders. My father did a great job of building two successful businesses during his lifetime in spite of war forcing him to reestablish his family and his company. A refugee doesn't have stability, but he and my mother always made sure we had a home even when we didn't have a country. My parents taught us home was wherever our family was together.

I created Hikma so I could show love and service to my family and my country, Jordan—and that's never stopped. Even though I've achieved many of my goals, I'm not through yet. I want to continue finding ways to improve the lives of my family, my employees, my customers, my local communities, the world, and future generations. Samira and I have always stressed the importance of looking out for others and helping those in need.

I hope my wife will always look forward to seeing me.

I hope my children and grandchildren will always remain ethical, independent, and courageous.

I hope Hikma's leaders and employees will always retain the values and corporate responsibility the company has had since the day I started it.

I hope my story of entrepreneurship will be an inspiration for younger generations—and for you. With hard work, a clear vision, and strong passion, anyone can be successful and make his or her dreams come true.

Also by the Author
Building a Global Success

Nice Guys Do Finish First

Samih T. Darwazah defied ALL the experts and reinvented the corporation. Using five thousand years of Middle Eastern wisdom and plenty of old-fashioned American values and know-how, he built a billion-dollar global company. And here's why that's important to you:

While today's CEOs slash salaries and benefits—when not engaged in wholesale firings and hiring cheap foreign labor—Darwazah put people first, respected his employees, emphasized research and invention, embraced education and invested in the United States. And he made money—lots of money. With his alternative principles and strategies to greed, ruthlessness, hypocrisy, poor quality and outsourcing to foreign countries, Darwazah proved nice guys not only finish first—they build billion-dollar companies.

What's more, Darwazah is a product of American foreign policy—a Fulbright Scholar and graduate of the American University of Beirut. He went from war refugee to the pinnacle of corporate power and political influence, with the ears of kings, queens and presidents. He has become one of the most liked, admired and emulated business leaders in the world. *Building a Global Success* reveals inside details about his life and business secrets spanning his fifty-plus years as a corporate and political power broker.

"Proves that the classically American business model—lean management, investing in 'human capital,' providing quality service and building the best products—remains a winning choice in this day and age of outsourcing, downsizing and bankruptcies."
—Professor John Quelch, senior associate dean, Harvard Business School

BUILDING A GLOBAL SUCCESS

The Story of Samih Darwazah and the Rise of Hikma

SAMIH T. DARWAZAH